The Impact of the Growth of the Sharing and Gig Economy on VAT/GST Policy and Administration

OECD
BETTER POLICIES FOR BETTER LIVES

Please cite this publication as:
OECD (2021), *The Impact of the Growth of the Sharing and Gig Economy on VAT/GST Policy and Administration*, OECD Publishing, Paris, *https://doi.org/10.1787/51825505-en*.

ISBN 978-92-64-79816-8 (print)
ISBN 978-92-64-91478-0 (pdf)

Photo credits: Cover © Shutterstock/PopTika.

Corrigenda to publications may be found on line at: *www.oecd.org/about/publishing/corrigenda.htm*.

Foreword

This report on "*The impact of the growth of the sharing and gig economy on VAT/GST policy and administration*" (hereafter the Report) is published as a further addition to the series of OECD reports and guidance on the design of VAT/GST policy to address the challenges of the digitalisation of the economy (most notably the 2019 Report on the Role of Digital platforms in the Collection of VAT/GST on Online Sales).

The emergence and rapid expansion of the so-called sharing/gig economy in recent years have been remarkable. It has been powered by the rise of digital platforms acting as intermediaries for millions of new economic actors and consumers worldwide. These have facilitated a socio-economic shift towards an on-demand-driven monetisation of (sometimes) underutilised human or physical resources and/or assets by making them accessible for temporary ("shared") use by consumers for a consideration.

A 2019 study (Mastercard and Kaiser Associates) covering the global major markets indicates that the sharing/gig economy has generated a gross value of USD 204 Billion in 2018 and is projected to reach a gross value of USD 455 billion by 2023 as digitalisation accelerates, and consumers are becoming even more receptive to the idea of sharing (Mastercard and Kaiser Associates, 2019[1]).

This exponential growth of sharing/gig economy activity has created a new commercial reality in a number of industries, particularly in the sectors of transportation (with the emergence of "ride-sourcing") and accommodation (particularly in short-term rentals). This new reality involves large groups of new economic actors carrying out commercial activities in new ways that may not yet be captured by existing VAT/GST rules and administrative practice. This may impact VAT/GST revenue and the competitive position of traditional business activity. Against this background, VAT/GST authorities from OECD as well as non-OECD countries, notably at the fifth meeting of the OECD Global Forum on VAT in 2019, made a strong call for work by the OECD to support an efficient and coordinated VAT/GST policy response to this new reality.

This Report presents the outcome of this work. Chapter 1 presents the key features and the main business models in the sharing/gig economy that are likely to be relevant from a VAT/GST perspective, and the possible VAT/GST challenges and opportunities associated with its growth. Chapter 2 provides a framework for the development of a VAT/GST strategy in response to the growth and development of the sharing/gig economy. Chapter 3 presents a range of VAT/GST measures to support an efficient and effective policy response to the challenges and opportunities of sharing/gig economy growth, in particular through the simplification of compliance processes, the collection and effective use of data and (alternative) VAT/GST collection approaches. This is complemented with detailed guidance on the potential roles of digital platforms in facilitating and enhancing VAT/GST compliance in the sharing/gig economy. Chapter 4 presents a number of compliance risk management and enforcement strategies for tax authorities to consider as part of their overall policy response. An in-depth analysis of the business models in the currently dominant sharing/gig economy sectors of accommodation and transportation is included in Annex D.

The Report does not aim at detailed prescriptions for national legislation. It is presented as a source of reference to assist tax authorities in assessing the VAT/GST implications of the sharing/gig economy and in identifying appropriate VAT/GST policy responses in light of their specific circumstances and policy priorities.

It has been developed under the auspices of the OECD Committee on Fiscal Affairs (CFA) via its Working Party No.9 on Consumption Taxes (WP9) and a dedicated Expert Group. It is the result of an inclusive process, through intense consultation with representatives from OECD members and from a considerable number of non-OECD countries via the Global Forum on VAT as well as with the representatives of key sharing/gig economy actors and academia through the Technical Advisory Group to WP9.

This report was approved by the Committee on Fiscal Affairs on 6 April 2021 and prepared for publication by the OECD Secretariat.

Table of contents

Tables

Figures

Executive Summary

The rise of the sharing and gig economy has fundamentally transformed a number of industries within just a few short years. Digital platforms have been at the centre of this (r)evolution. Continuous technological advancements, not least the ability to collect and analyse vast amounts of data, have allowed digital platforms to successfully implement innovative business models that have created "new ways of doing things", based on the sharing of assets (goods and services) rather than on traditional ownership-based concepts. This transformation reflects consumers' growing preference for more flexible on-demand access to assets and services, particularly among younger people, and the interest of private individuals and businesses in the opportunities this creates to monetize (under)utilized assets and labour.

Digital platforms' success in facilitating the growth of the sharing/gig economy and in further stimulating and diversifying it, has already disrupted the sectors of transportation, tourism and hospitality, professional services and finance. New sharing/gig economy entrants have fundamentally challenged the position of long-established traditional players. And this is expected to be only the beginning. Traditional players are entering the platforms economy, benefitting from the potential it offers to restore and/or generate demand at relatively low cost. Meanwhile, any other industry can potentially face change from the emergence of sharing models.

This transformative change creates challenges for regulatory frameworks across a range of areas, including for Value Added Taxes/Goods and Services Taxes (VAT/GST). Sharing/gig economy growth has triggered the entry into the market of considerable, and still growing, numbers of new economic actors carrying out activities in often new ways and with a non-standard employment or work status.

This has raised questions whether existing VAT/GST frameworks are sufficiently equipped to capture this new economic reality efficiently, notably to protect VAT/GST revenue and minimise economic distortions. It also raises the question whether this "new way of doing things", not least the role of sharing/gig economy platforms, creates new opportunities to enhance compliance and administration.

This Report shows that there is no single, definitive, one-size-fits-all response to these questions. Policy responses are likely to differ across sectors and jurisdictions, notably in light of existing VAT/GST policy and administration frameworks. Sharing/gig economy growth is also still in its early stages, although it has already fundamentally transformed a number of industries, and it is still continuously changing and evolving.

Against this background, this Report sets out the core components of a comprehensive strategy for tax authorities to consider in designing and implementing their VAT/GST policy and administration response to sharing/gig economy growth. It reflects consensus among representatives from VAT/GST authorities worldwide and from key industry stakeholders, based on intense and inclusive analysis, consultation and experience sharing. In summary, these core components are as follows:

- Acquiring the necessary understanding of sharing/gig economy activity, its main actors and business models, its main sectors, its size and growth potential. To support this assessment, a unique analysis of the currently dominant sharing/gig economy sectors of accommodation and transportation is included in this Report;

- Assessing the need for VAT/GST policy action, if any, and its objectives (the "why" question). These are likely to include the protection of VAT/GST revenues and/or the potential to broadening the VAT/GST base, and minimising risks of competitive distortion;
- Determining and implementing the appropriate VAT/GST policy and administration responses (the "how" question). These are likely to involve a role for sharing/gig economy platforms in sharing data and/or collecting the VAT/GST. In addition, a range of policy and administration measures can be considered to facilitate and simplify compliance for sharing/gig economy providers.

In discussing these components for a VAT/GST strategy in response to sharing/gig economy growth, and in providing guidance for their design and implementation, this Report notably presents the following findings and observations:

- **Jurisdictions' main objective may not necessarily be to bring all sharing/gig economy activities within the VAT/GST net.** A jurisdiction may for instance wish to first monitor evolutions across sharing/gig economy sectors so as to allow fast and targeted policy action when needed.
- **Jurisdictions may opt for a sequenced strategy**, focusing their policy action first on the dominant sharing/gig economy sectors that may create the most immediate risks to VAT/GST revenue and/or competitive neutrality.
- **The preferred policy response is one that is consistent with the general rules and principles of the jurisdiction's existing VAT/GST system and limits the introduction of new exceptions or special regimes**. This notably reflects the desire of jurisdictions to ensuring an equal treatment of various distribution channels in a given market, be they traditional or digital.
- **Tax authorities will often face the difficult trade-off between the need to protect revenue and minimise competitive distortion, and the need to safeguard the efficiency of tax administration and to avoid undue compliance burden**. The latter may point to an approach that minimizes the entry of high numbers of new sharing/gig economy actors into the VAT/GST system, perhaps with limited compliance capacity and knowledge of their tax obligations. The revenue and competitive consequences of this approach may be significant, when activity shifts from a limited number of established and largely VAT/GST compliant traditional operators to a large number of small sharing/gig economy operators that may remain outside the scope of VAT/GST (e.g. hotel activity vs. short-term vacation rentals). Bringing these new sharing/gig economy operators into the VAT/GST net may on the other hand create undue pressure on tax administration and compliance challenges for operators.
- **To support a balanced response to this challenge, this Report sets out a number possible measures aimed at managing the number of new economic actors entering the VAT/GST system, and at simplifying compliance obligations for sharing/gig economy providers.** These include: considerations for the determination of a VAT/GST registration and/or collection threshold; presumptive schemes for determining the VAT/GST liability; accounting and reporting simplifications; split payment/withholding mechanisms for VAT/GST collection; the use of technology to facilitate VAT/GST administration and compliance; third-party reporting obligations; taxpayer education and other awareness raising activities.
- **The Report highlights the significant opportunities created by the central role of digital platforms in sharing/gig economy activity and growth, fuelled by advanced data analytics, in facilitating VAT/GST administration and compliance.** It considers approaches for the implementation of data reporting obligations notably leveraging on the 2020 OECD Model Rules for Reporting by Platform Operators with respect to Sellers in the Sharing/gig Economy; the collection of VAT/GST by sharing/gig economy on the sharing/gig economy supplies that they

facilitate; and approaches to educating sharing/gig economy providers on their VAT/GST obligations.

- **In presenting these policy options, this Report points at the considerable opportunities created by the role of digital platforms and big data, for greater visibility and traceability of economic activity and for formalisation of previously informal economic activity particularly in developing economies.**
- **The Report finally presents a number of supporting measures for the efficient and effective operation of these policy options,** including targeted risk management strategies through extensive use of third party data to assist compliance **monitoring** and data analysis; deterrents for non-compliance; and/or robust international administrative co-operation as appropriate.

1 Exploring the VAT/GST implications of the sharing/gig economy as part of the platform economy – a broad perspective

This chapter provides the overall context of this report, most notably the explosive growth of the sharing/gig economy, its key features and the main business models that are considered relevant from a VAT/GST perspective, and the associated possible VAT/GST challenges and opportunities. It also describes the objective and the scope of this report.

1.1. Introduction

The digitalisation of the economy via advanced technology has transformed the way people supply and consume goods and services. Particularly, the emergence of a so-called 'sharing/gig economy' signals a paradigm shift from ownership to the temporary access-based use of human or physical resources and/or assets, primarily by and among individuals for a consideration.

While the notion of 'sharing' assets and/or resources as a socio-economic model may not be entirely new, the recent technological developments, notably the rise of digital platforms that provide advanced technological solutions and trust building tools, have dramatically facilitated the expansion of the sharing/gig economy by increasing the accessibility to these assets and resources and the capability of users to transact with each other with great flexibility, trust and convenience and also by reducing information asymmetries and various transaction costs.

The prominent role of digital platforms in the sharing/gig economy has been recognised by the 2019 OECD report on the *Role of Digital Platforms in the Collection of VAT/GST on Online Sales* (the 2019 Digital Platforms report) (OECD, 2019[1]), which provides practical guidance to tax authorities on the design and implementation of a variety of solutions for digital platforms in the effective and efficient collection of VAT/GST on online sales. The 2019 Digital Platforms report acknowledged however that, within the platform economy, the sharing/gig economy has specific characteristics that required further evaluation and analysis (OECD, 2019[1]).

The exponential growth of the sharing/gig economy activity as facilitated by the digital platforms has revolutionised the commercial reality in a number of sectors, particularly in transportation (with the emergence of "ride-sourcing") and accommodation (particularly short-term (vacation) rental) sectors. This new reality, involving large groups of new economic actors carrying out their commercial activities in new ways that may not yet be captured by traditional tax rules and administrative practice, may impact VAT/GST revenue, policy design and administration and the competitive position of traditional business activity.

Given the need to further evaluate the issue and to consult with relevant stakeholders on the role(s) of sharing/gig economy platforms in the VAT/GST compliance process in respect of the sharing/gig economy supplies, the OECD Working Party No.9 on Consumption Taxes (WP9) consisting of VAT/GST policy officials from OECD members and Partner countries, signalled a need to develop work in this area as a separate work stream. This work was expected to consider the sharing/gig economy within the context of the broader platform economy and to consider specific features and aspects that may affect the design and operation of the roles for digital platforms in the collection of VAT/GST as presented in the 2019 Digital Platforms report (OECD, 2019[1]).

This request for further OECD work in this area was widely echoed at the meeting of the Global Forum on VAT in March 2019, where tax authorities from around the world expressed the urgent need for work by the OECD on the VAT/GST treatment of the sharing/gig economy. Participants flagged the potentially significant impact on VAT/GST revenue, on tax administration and on the competitive position of traditional business activity as key drivers for this work. This call for work on the VAT/GST treatment of the sharing/gig economy was strongly supported by Business at OECD, through its membership in the Technical Advisory Group to WP9 (TAG). The OECD's Committee on Fiscal Affairs (CFA) and the OECD Council confirmed the importance of this work by including it as a priority in the CFA's Programme of Work and Budget for 2019-20.

Against this background, the OECD has developed this report with the active involvement of all relevant key stakeholders, including the business community and countries beyond the OECD membership via the Global Forum on VAT.

1.1.1. The objective of this report

It is recognised that the sharing/gig economy gives rise to a variety of economic, social, tax, legal and regulatory questions beyond VAT/GST policy design and administration and compliance. While this report considers the possible impact of these various aspects on VAT/GST policy and administration and vice-versa, where appropriate, it focuses exclusively on the VAT/GST aspects.

Accordingly, the overall objective of this report is to enhance tax authorities' understanding of the sharing/gig economy from an economic and commercial perspective, identify and analyse the opportunities and challenges it creates for VAT/GST policy and administration and to suggest the possible policy approaches and measures that tax authorities could consider in this context.

The underlying assumption is that tax authorities may wish to monitor and consider the VAT/GST implications of the sharing/gig economy in light of their specific circumstances and policy objective(s). The policy objective may not necessarily be to bring (all) sharing/gig economy supplies within the VAT/GST net.

This report does not aim at prescription for national legislation. Jurisdictions are sovereign with respect to the design and application of their laws. Rather, the report seeks to enhance jurisdictions' understanding of this evolving phenomenon and assist the tax authorities in evaluating and developing possible policy responses to address the VAT/GST implications of the growth of the sharing/gig economy, with particular guidance to maximising the effectiveness of such measures and to the extent possible their consistency across jurisdictions. International consistency will assist to facilitate compliance, lower compliance costs and administrative burdens and improve the effectiveness of the VAT/GST systems, recognising in particular that a number of the sharing/gig economy actors, notably digital platforms, are likely to be faced with multi-jurisdictional obligations.

Considering the sharing/gig economy as part of the broader platform economy but with specific characteristics, this report complements the 2019 Digital Platforms report (OECD, 2019[1]). It intends to be evolutionary in nature, notably in light of the rapid development of technology and a wide range of activities involved and their delivery processes.

1.1.2. The scope of this report

This report discusses the key features of the sharing/gig economy and its business models that are likely to be relevant from a VAT/GST perspective and presents a range of possible policy responses to address the impact of sharing/gig economy growth on VAT/GST policy and administration. These responses include potential roles for digital platforms involved in the sharing/gig economy supply chain as well as broader policy and administration options.

In evaluating available VAT/GST policy approaches against the key VAT/GST relevant features of the sharing/gig economy, this report takes into account the potential policy objectives pursued by a jurisdiction as well as the desirability for a jurisdiction to consider the *Ottawa Taxation Framework Conditions*, notably in respect of neutrality, efficiency, certainty and simplicity, effectiveness and fairness, and flexibility in framing and implementing the policy and administrative measures.

The report relies as appropriate on the *International VAT/GST Guidelines* (OECD, 2017[2]) and other relevant OECD work in response to the digitalisation of the economy, notably the 2019 Digital Platforms report (OECD, 2019[1]) and the 2020 *Model Rules for Reporting by Platform Operators with respect to Sellers in the Sharing and Gig Economy* (OECD, 2020[3]). Experience and analysis in jurisdictions that have taken VAT/GST measures in respect of the sharing/gig economy or that consider doing so, have informed this work and vice versa, as part of the ongoing sharing of analysis and experience.

While recognising that the growth of the sharing/gig economy may create different VAT/GST pressures, depending on the sector as well as jurisdictions' market structure and their VAT/GST system, evidence suggests that the accommodation and transportation sectors currently create the most urgent pressure on VAT/GST policy in jurisdictions worldwide and are therefore likely to require the most urgent and/or most extensive policy and/or administrative action from a VAT/GST perspective. The accommodation and transportation sectors are therefore used as pilot sectors for the analysis of the operation of the sharing/gig economy, respectively based on the sharing of assets and the sharing of labour (see further Annex D to this report). The analysis of these two sectors is expected to be helpful in informing the analysis in respect of the other sharing/gig economy sectors as appropriate.

The report endeavours to use neutral terminology rather than terminology that may already be used in specific jurisdictions or may have a different meaning across jurisdictions. It is important, therefore, for jurisdictions to take account of the broad meaning of the terms used in this report.

The report does not try to define the term "sharing/gig economy" as it is a concept that is likely to evolve over time. A number of different terms have been used in the literature as well as by jurisdictions that have either implemented policy actions to address the VAT/GST implications in this area, or are considering doing so. It has resulted in a unique set of nuances and challenges, not least for policy makers trying to measure its size and impact and identifying appropriate policy responses. Hence the report uses the term "sharing/gig economy" as a generic term to refer to part of the platform economy that has a number of specific features that are considered relevant from a VAT/GST perspective. Considering such specific features and building on already available definitions, a broad (working) description is used as a placeholder for the purposes of this report to refer to the sharing/gig economy as: "*An accessibility-based socio economic model, typically enabled or facilitated via advanced technological solutions and trust-building tools, whereby human or physical resources and/or assets are accessible (for temporary use)/shared – to a large extent – among individuals for either monetary or non-monetary benefits or a combination of both*".

In general, sharing economy activities notably involve the temporary substitution of ownership of (sometimes) underutilised assets/resources as opposed to the transfer of ownership such as sharing of one's apartment for short-term (vacation) rental purposes or sharing of a tool (equipment) for a manual work. Gig activities are in principle aimed at providing opportunities to a (high or low) skilled labour force to provide labour and/or professional services in the context of a labour market characterised by the prevalence of short-term and often non-standard contracts or freelance work as opposed to permanent jobs and standard labour contracts (c.f. *Tax Challenges Arising from Digitalisation – Interim report 2018* of the OECD/G20 Base Erosion and Profit Shifting Project (OECD, 2018[4])). These gig activities could include cleaning, gardening or more intellectual services such as web design, IT services and consultancy. The distinction between sharing and gig categories is not always clear-cut (e.g. the case of a driver that has spare capacity in his/her car and offers to take passengers who want to travel to the same direction for a fee). Sharing/gig economy actors may often offer a mix of asset and labour sharing activities.

This report recognises that the VAT/GST status of sharing/gig economy actors (including platforms and underlying providers) in a given jurisdiction will generally be determined by that jurisdiction's normal VAT/GST rules, often on a case-by-case basis in light of specific facts and circumstances. This includes the question whether a sharing/gig economy platform acts as a principal or as an agent for VAT/GST purposes (see Box 1.2. below). The new main challenges for VAT/GST policy and administration result from the large numbers of new economic actors that may enter the VAT/GST system as a result of sharing/gig economy growth. These new actors may often have a limited VAT/GST knowledge and/or capacity to comply (i.e. micro-businesses, SMEs) while their activities may involve considerable VAT/GST revenues and create risks of competitive distortion that are limited at an individual level but may be significant at an aggregated level. The aim of this report is primarily to identify and analyse these challenges and to present a range of possible options for tax policy and administration to address them.

1.2. Understanding the sharing/gig economy as part of the platform economy – a high-level introduction

1.2.1. The rapid growth of the sharing/gig economy on a global and regional level

The rapid growth of the sharing/gig economy is a global phenomenon. A range of major sharing/gig economy platforms are operating across multiple jurisdictions worldwide. As the sharing/gig economy continues to evolve, and given the complexity and variation of the platforms and activities involved, there are not yet a great deal of data available that provide a reliable insight into its true size. The collection of statistical data to measure its size, growth and activity has proven to be challenging but efforts are being made to develop a framework and methodology to improve the measurement of the sharing/gig economy. Despite these difficulties, available evidence suggests that the sharing/gig economy has significantly grown and expanded globally in recent years with significant potential for further growth in the future. A 2019 study covering the major markets around the world suggests that sharing/gig economy activity was worth USD 204 billion in 2018 and is projected to reach USD 455 billion by 2023 as consumers are becoming more receptive to the idea of sharing and as digitalisation accelerates (Mastercard and Kaiser Associates, 2019[5]).[1]

The sharing/gig economy is constantly evolving. The Covid-19 pandemic (see Annex B for further analysis) together with other developments in the regulatory domain (e.g. developments in labour law that could reshape the relations between the platforms and their providers) and in the technological landscape (e.g. the potential use of self-driving cars in the future) could transform the scope and scale of the sharing/gig economy both at national and global level. Hence there is a need for continuous monitoring of developments in this area.

Emerging key sectors of the sharing/gig economy

Given its versatile nature, the sharing/gig economy can potentially involve a wide range of activities across different sectors of the economy. Box 1.1. below describes the four emerging key sectors of the sharing/gig economy.

Box 1.1. Emerging key sectors of the sharing/gig economy

- **Transportation sector**: typically, the platform connects drivers, who may be non-professional in the sense that they may not possess professional permits (e.g. taxi medallion) other than a legitimate driver's license, with passengers, often private individuals, for either a short or long distance trip. It is noted that jurisdictions increasingly implement measures that require drivers to obtain professional permits to operate, notably in an online ride-sourcing context (see further in Annex D).
- **Accommodation sector**: typically, the platform connects potential guests with professional or non-professional hosts offering accommodation services. Increasingly, the platform may offer other services such as air travel, car rentals and vacation experience either on their own name or on behalf of other platforms and/or third parties (see further in Annex D).
- **On-demand services sector**: typically, the platform enables (often) private individuals to locate high or low-skilled labour force with spare capacity to provide labour and/or professional services. The services could include (skilled) manual work such as cleaning, moving, carpentry that mostly involve physical delivery and professional services such as web design, consultancy, legal, IT, data entry, 'click-work' that mostly involve digital delivery.
- **Collaborative finance, including crowdfunding, lending and donations**: typically, the platform connects individuals and businesses to invest, lend and borrow money directly between and from each other without the involvement of traditional financial institutions such as banks. These mainly include crowdfunding platforms and peer-to-peer lending platforms (either individual-to-individual consumer lending or investor to SMEs and/or start-ups lending).

Source: OECD research based on public sources

Among these sectors, evidence suggests that the accommodation and transportation sectors are the two largest sectors in terms of total transaction value. These sectors collectively represent approximately 90% of the total sharing/gig economy market value globally (see Figure 1.1. below).

It is projected that the growth rates of the current two largest sectors (i.e. transportation and accommodation) will remain high in the coming years as these two sectors continue leading the market. Sub-business models in the transportation sector, such as the delivery model (e.g. food delivery; shopping delivery), are also expected to grow rapidly as major ride-sourcing platforms are continuing to expand into these areas, leveraging their well-established network of drivers to differentiate their service offerings (see further description of sub-business models in Annex D). The professional services sector and the crowdfunding/lending sector are two other sectors with considerable growth expectations.

Figure 1.1. Sharing/gig economy volume by sector (Billions USD, 2018)

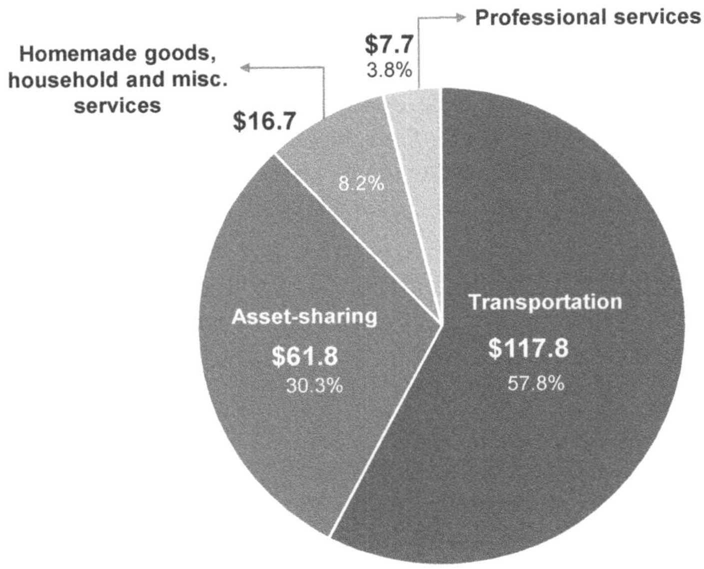

Note: The markets covered include Australia, Brazil, France, India, Indonesia, United Arab Emirates, United Kingdom and the United States.
Source: The Global Gig Economy: Capitalizing on a ~$500B Opportunity (2019) by Mastercard and Kaiser Associates (Mastercard and Kaiser Associates, 2019[5])

The sharing/gig economy in emerging economies

The sharing/gig economy is also in full expansion in the developing world where it is often very visible in daily life. A global survey conducted by Nielsen in 2014 indicated that people in developing countries are more receptive to the idea of sharing assets than those in developed regions: Asia-Pacific (78%); Latin America (70%); Middle East Africa (68%); Europe (54%) and North America (52%) (Nielsen, 2014[6]).

Evidence suggests that developing markets represent greater potential for gig economy growth in particular, in light of the often significant interest for freelance ("gig") work among their growing populations. Paired with increasing mobile phone penetration and rising digital banking access, such emerging economies are projected to represent a greater portion of the global gig economy in the future with their accelerating freelancer participation rates (Mastercard and Kaiser Associates, 2019[5]).

The dominant sectors of the sharing/gig economy businesses operating in low and middle-income countries include motorbike taxi services; connecting freelance workers with potential clients; agriculture-related activities, notably involving the sharing of information on crop prices, agricultural disease risks and treatments, or the sharing of agricultural equipment and storage or processing facilities (e.g. by connecting farmers who own tractors with farmers in need of them).

While global platform giants that operate across multiple countries are also expanding their services in developing economies, some of the typical sharing/gig economy platform services have been replicated locally, and regionally dominant platforms have emerged, catering for region-specific needs and circumstances.

1.2.2. Drivers of the sharing/gig economy

The recent proliferation of the sharing/gig economy activities in the past decade has been largely driven by the advances in technology, enabled to a large extent by digital platforms that offer enormous potential to scale fast, increase the scope and frequency of transactions with reduced transaction costs and increased accessibility combined with enhanced trust assurance and ease of connection and payment.

In addition to the technological developments, available studies and evidence suggest that there are various social and economic factors that drive the growth of the sharing/gig economy. One key factor is the high market demand, i.e. consumers' interest in the sharing/gig economy products/services and the desire to monetise (under)utilised existing uses of assets that has attracted significant levels of private funding especially in certain sectors e.g. ride-sourcing.

Another factor is the changing economic behaviour, notably in the aftermath of a financial and economic crisis, whereby people are seeking ways to save and earn supplemental income while embracing a more "flexible" work-life environment. This attitude is more profound amongst younger people. Evidence shows that individuals providing labour-intensive services are typically from the lower end of the income spectrum, while those providing capital-intensive services have higher average monthly incomes.

In addition, the absence of (adapted/targeted) regulation may play a role. One of the drivers for the growing popularity of the sharing/gig economy is arguably the low barrier to enter the sharing/gig economy, notably as a consequence of the absence of (adapted/targeted) regulation, allowing consumers and providers to switch roles easily and quickly. This means in practice that individuals may easily opt for a regular (full-time) activity, making the sharing/gig economy activities their primary source of income, or irregularly at a lower frequency (part-time) to supplement other income. This flexibility to determine when to supply services can be of great value, as it reduces the opportunity cost of working and increases efficiency. It may have positive well-being effects by allowing sharing/gig economy participants to work a few more hours or renting out an asset, and thus loosen their budget constraints and expand their opportunities.

Other social factors could include increased environmental concerns. People may consider the sharing of underutilised assets as an effective way to reduce waste and to engage in a more environmentally friendly and sustainable economy. Moreover, people may associate the sharing/gig economy with social initiatives, such as empowering communities and improving access to a variety of goods, services, and facilities that would otherwise be unavailable or restricted to large businesses or high income households. Development of a sharing mentality among younger people is an additional factor driving the change.

1.2.3. Business models operated by digital platforms in the sharing/gig economy – An overview

As indicated before, digital platforms are at the forefront of sharing/gig economy development and growth as they employ advanced technology to connect providers and users of a continuously growing variety of sharing/gig economy services. The digital platforms involved in the sharing/gig economy activities cover a broad spectrum, ranging from small start-ups focusing on a specific niche to global giants. New sharing/gig economy platforms are continuously emerging and their business models continue to evolve. Even within the same sector, variations of different business models may operate.

Figure 1.2. below illustrates four typical business models operated by sharing/gig economy platforms categorized on the basis of their "control" and "rivalry" dimensions as follows:

- *The "control element", i*.e. the level of control exercised by the platform operator (e.g. whether the platform dictates the terms of the service delivery), will often differ among platforms. For example, a platform may exercise a high degree of control over the entire service delivery (e.g. acting in the name of the provider or reselling the service, managing content and sales, matching providers with users through a centralised app, dictate the price); or the platform may exercise a loose control and act more like an overseer of the platform rather than a supervisor, in which case the platform controls the user experience on the platform, but the underlying supply and its terms are controlled by and contracted between the provider and the user. It orchestrates the participants' efforts and it gains a competitive advantage by cultivating long-term relationships with supply-side participants. Despite the differences in business models, all platforms appear to exercise control to some extent as it is in their own interest to streamline the services to facilitate the transaction and create optimal experience for customers.

- Additionally, *the "rivalry element", i.e.* the degree to which a market mechanism operates in the platform, may also differ among platforms. For example, users may be allowed to set their own prices based on recommendation by the platform algorithm that takes into account supply and demand; or prices may be set on the basis of a dynamic pricing algorithm that reflects changes in supply and demand, or on the basis of predefined categories rather than on dynamic adjustments. The providers may be obliged to apply prices as determined by the platform (typically used by ride-sharing/car-pooling platforms).

Figure 1.2. Four business models of the sharing/gig economy platforms

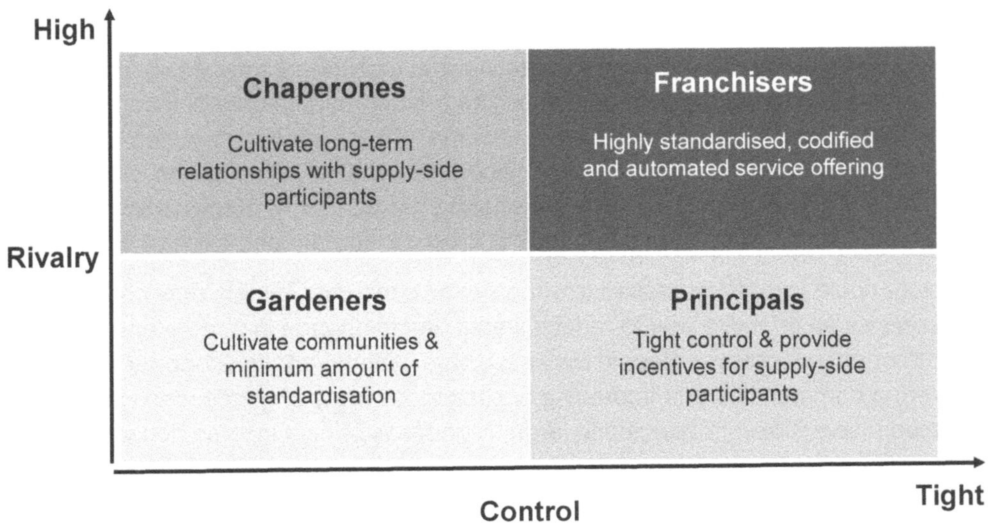

Source: Four Models of Sharing Economy Platforms (2017) by MIS Quarterly Executive (Constantiou, 2017[7])

From a VAT/GST policy perspective, it may be useful to note that these variations in business models within sectors may have an impact on the degree of control that a platform operator exercises over the supply/users of the platform; the information collected by or available to the platform; the payment flows for the sharing/gig activities facilitated by the platform. Annex D provides a more detailed description of the business models operated by the major platforms in the two largest sharing/gig economy sectors, i.e. the accommodation and transportation sectors, including the key features of these platforms and functions performed.

Evolution and convergence *of business models*

Increasingly, as digital platforms operating in the sharing/gig economy scale up, it is not uncommon to see a platform facilitating a variety of services based on different business models. For example, a ride-sourcing platform may facilitate a ride-sharing/car-pooling service, matching drivers with passengers going in the same direction and sharing the costs of the ride. Equally, some platforms, notably in the accommodation sector, are facilitating platform-to-platform supplies that allow the host platform to provide (an access to) a wider range of offerings by other platforms or third parties to the final consumer.

At the same time, another important trend observed is the ongoing convergence between sharing/gig economy activities and business models and the broader (traditional and platforms) economy. In order to remain competitive, traditional economic operators that are faced with competition from sharing/gig economy operators have started adjusting and expanding their offering to compete with this new reality. This could include launching their own applications on existing platforms, launching competing platforms and/or acquiring existing platforms. In addition to creating online distribution channels to compete with sharing/gig economy platforms, traditional operators may also differentiate their service offerings. Existing hotel brands have for instance started to offer apartment and homestays. Similarly, sharing/gig economy platforms continue to expand their services and are starting to resemble their traditional counterparts in certain cases (e.g. platforms in the accommodation sector moving towards owning and controlling accommodation). At the same time, sharing/gig activity may create new capacity, e.g. people acquiring assets with the sole purpose of offering them for short-term rental through a platform instead of using underutilised assets. These trends may gradually reduce the difference between sharing/gig economy actors and other economic operators in the traditional and/or the broader platform economy.

1.3. Mapping the possible VAT/GST implications of the sharing/gig economy

It is recognised that the sharing/gig economy gives rise to a variety of economic, social, tax, legal and regulatory questions beyond the area of VAT/GST administration and compliance. The analysis in this report, however, focuses exclusively on the VAT/GST implications of sharing/gig economy growth, thereby taking account of evolutions in these various other areas on VAT/GST policy and administration and vice-versa, where appropriate.

To further analyse the VAT/GST implications of the sharing/gig economy, section 1.3.1. below first further explores and distils the specific features of the sharing/gig economy that are relevant for VAT/GST policy design and administration. Section 1.3.2. considers the main actors in a sharing/gig economy supply chain and analyses their interactions that are likely to be relevant from a VAT/GST perspective. This is complemented with a sectoral typology based on the key operational features of sharing/gig economy activities in Section 1.3.3. The broad VAT/GST opportunities and challenges associated with sharing/gig economy growth are finally analysed in Sections 1.3.4. and 1.3.5., in light of what is discussed in the preceding sections.

1.3.1. Key features of the sharing/gig economy that are relevant for VAT/GST policy design and administration

As the sharing/gig economy continues to evolve rapidly and new business models emerge and converge with existing business models, it is increasingly difficult to draw the line between sharing/gig economy activities and other activities in the broader economy. Nevertheless, the sharing/gig economy has specific characteristics compared to the broader platform economy that merit further evaluation and analysis from a VAT/GST perspective.

Digital platforms are at the forefront of sharing/gig economy growth, by connecting providers and users through advanced technological solutions and trust-building tools such as online reviews, reputation mechanisms and secure online payment systems (see Annex D for a further overview of platform features). For the digital platforms involved in the sharing/gig economy, these tools are essential features as the need for quality assurance, verification, optimisation of customer experience and payment security is crucial for their success.

The underlying activities in the sharing/gig economy are generally not new (e.g. transport services, accommodation rentals), but the rise of sharing/gig economy platforms powered by digital technology has enabled their scale, scope and frequency to reach an unprecedented scale at global level. Some of these activities may have been typically untaxed or non-taxable under existing VAT/GST regimes (e.g. the exploitation of an asset by a private individual). The scope of these sharing/gig activities is potentially limitless as long as technology is capable of supporting interactions between providers and interested customers.

Sharing/gig economy providers are often private individuals[2] that may carry out high numbers of low-value ("micro") transactions, particularly in gig economy sectors such as transportation (ride-sourcing). These individual providers may undertake the sharing/gig economy activities to supplement their primary source of income and their engagement may thus be of an infrequent/occasional nature and be spread across multiple platforms.

These providers may often use assets that they also use partly for private purposes. These (private individual) providers are often likely to have no or limited knowledge of VAT/GST obligations and may not have the capacity to comply with these obligations even if they are aware of them. Moreover, the profile and status of sharing/gig economy providers is diverse and in constant evolution. While private individuals acting in a self-employed capacity with an often higher-than-average level of income volatility may represent a large share of sharing/gig economy providers, it does not exclude that their activities may just as easily be performed by individuals that have incorporated their business activity and/or that are less exposed to income volatility, or that these providers' relationship with a platform evolves to one that may become akin to an employer-employee relationship under some business models (These aspects are further considered in section 1.3.2 below).

Platform technology allows these providers to easily access large numbers of potential customers with no or minimal upfront investment. The sharing/gig economy can thus potentially transform a large number of individuals operating through a platform into businesses (possibly with global coverage) that can collectively compete with the (largest) traditional economic operators. For example, the large numbers of private individuals that are now offering their property for short-term rental via accommodation platforms have become real competitors for the traditional hotel sector. The line between a private individual and a business thus becomes increasingly difficult to draw.

Sharing/gig economy platforms may often have no physical presence in the jurisdiction where the transactions that they facilitate are carried out (performed and/or used or consumed). The providers of the sharing/gig economy activities generally have a presence in the jurisdiction where these activities are performed and/or carried out. This presence may involve the physical presence of the provider in the taxing jurisdiction (e.g. driver's presence in the ride-sourcing sector) or may be limited to the presence of provider's assets in the taxing jurisdiction (e.g. immovable property of a certain value to be located in the taxing jurisdiction). Providers may temporarily move across jurisdictions to engage in sharing/gig economy activities (e.g. frontier workers or people who stay in a jurisdiction for a couple of months to undertake a sharing/gig economy activities) even though these cases are rare. While users and providers of sharing/gig economy activities may often both have a physical presence in the jurisdiction where these activities are performed and/or consumed at the time of this performance or consumption (e.g. the transportation services or the short-term rental), this is not necessarily always the case (notably where services can be provided remotely) and providers and users may have their usual residence or business establishment in different jurisdictions.

Sharing/gig economy activities generally involve the (temporary) use of resources (assets and/or labour) without involving any transfer of ownership of assets. These activities could involve renting, swapping and sharing of assets; either for a fee or against compensation of the cost of the activity proportionate to the use of the asset (cost-sharing arrangements). Sharing/gig economy activities may also be performed for a non-monetary consideration (i.e. in-kind compensation).

Certain types of the sharing/gig economy activity may however no longer involve the "sharing" of excess capacity as described above but evolve towards a more traditional type of service activity, facilitated by a digital platform. Take the example of a driver who leases out a car that (s)he did not have before in order to offer rides, versus a driver that may have spare capacity in his/her car and plan on driving particular route with passengers who want to travel on the same route. The same is true for (underutilised) assets in the accommodation sector: it may become increasingly less clear whether a short-term rental activity relates to a (temporarily) underutilised property, or whether the property has for instance been acquired as an investment and is predominantly offered for short-term rental.

Payments in the sharing/gig economy are typically made through electronic means of payment (e.g. credit cards, e-banking, bitcoins, etc.) with or without the involvement the platforms (payment processing can be outsourced to third parties). This widespread usage of electronic means of payment could enhance the access to data to facilitate the tracing and monitoring of sharing/gig economy activities and/or to relevant data for VAT/GST compliance in respect of the sharing/gig economy supplies (incl. to support platforms taking on these compliance obligations on behalf of the sharing/gig economy suppliers). Evidence suggests that cash payments are still accepted in certain sectors and/or by certain operators, especially in developing economies.

1.3.2. Identifying the key actors/interactions that may be relevant from a VAT/GST perspective – A basic scenario of the sharing/gig economy supply chain

Determining the role/status of the actors involved in the sharing/gig economy supply chain is an important element when considering the VAT/GST treatment of a sharing/gig economy supply. Building on the key VAT/GST relevant features of the sharing/gig economy, Box 1.2. below provides an illustration of a basic scenario of the sharing/gig economy supply chain and potential interactions among the key sharing/gig economy actors with additional considerations from a VAT/GST perspective.

Box 1.2. A basic scenario of the sharing and gig economy supply chain - typical interactions among the key sharing/gig economy actors that may be relevant from a VAT/GST perspective

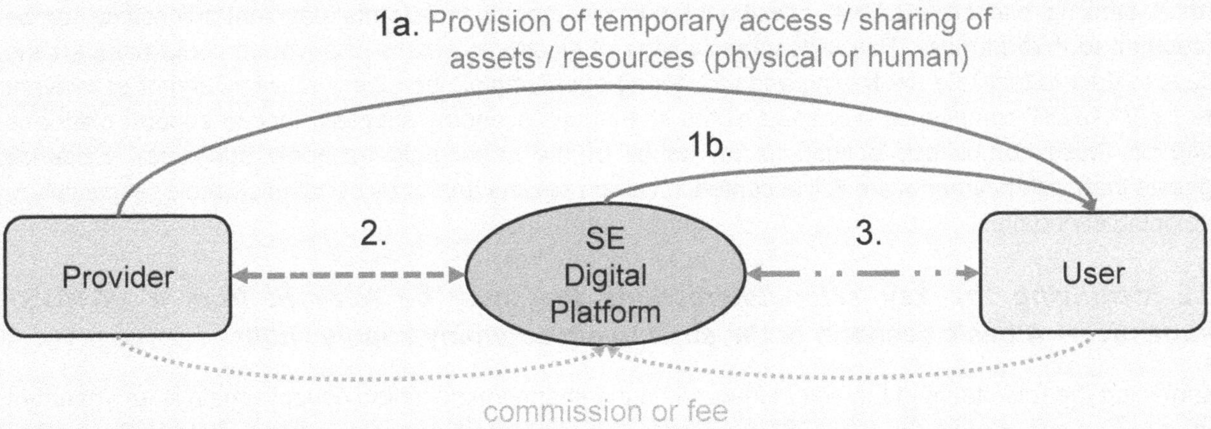

Possible interactions among the parties may include:

1a. Provision of temporary access/sharing of assets/resources (physical or human) by the provider to the user

1b. Provision of temporary access/sharing of assets/resources (physical or human) by the digital platform to the user

2. Interaction between the provider and the digital platform

3. Interaction between the digital platform and the user

Note: the sequence of numbers assigned in the diagram is for identification only. It is not intended to indicate the timing of a specific step in chronological order.
Source: OECD analysis.

Although there are many different sectors in which sharing/gig economy platforms operate, and their business models vary, a sharing/gig economy transaction will typically involve the following different group of actors/participants, which may not necessarily be located in the same jurisdiction:

- The provider[1] (often a private individual) who shares assets, resources, time and/or skills in exchange for a consideration/fee (monetary);
- The user of these assets, resources, time and/or skills. Often the user is a private individual, but users with a business status cannot be excluded particularly in certain sectors (e.g. the accommodation and/or on-demand services sectors).
- The sharing/gig economy platform (SE Digital Platform) that enables access to advanced technology and trust building tools and allows providers to be connected with other users for the provision of sharing/gig economy supplies, directly or indirectly, to such users. Several terms may be used at national level to denominate these actors, including: “platforms”, “(online) marketplaces”, “electronic interfaces” or “intermediaries”.

With respect to the role of the digital platform in the supply chain, two main broad scenarios can be distinguished:

- Under scenario 1 (illustrated with arrow 1a on the diagram), the sharing/gig economy platform directly connects the provider(s) and the user(s) with respect to a sharing/gig economy supply. In return, the digital platform may receive a consideration/fee from either the provider or the user or both (**the "agent role"**).

- Under scenario 2 (illustrated with arrow 1b on the diagram), the platform first acquires the sharing/gig economy supply from the (underlying) provider and then it provides it in its own name to its user(s). Under this scenario, the platform is regarded by national legislation as the supplier of the service (**the "principal role"**). Often, these platforms contract with the individual underlying provider and they act as the contracting party to provide the service.

In determining the exact role/status of the digital platform and the underlying providers, it is recognised that national labour law may have an impact. This is particularly the case where the platform is considered to have a legal or *de facto* employment relationship with the (underlying) provider under national labour law. Under such circumstances, the platform may be considered as having provided the supply in its own name and on its own behalf (i.e. acting as principal) and the underlying provider may be considered as an employee.

Other actors can also be involved in the supply chain of a sharing/gig economy activity, with direct or indirect connection to the digital platform and/or the provider and/or the user. For example, in the food (meal) delivery activities, different providers may be involved in the preparation of the meal and subsequently in the delivery of the meal to the customer. In the accommodation sector, an agent may directly interact with a platform with respect to the listing of apartments that may belong to different owners who are not necessarily known to the platform.

[1] Even though the sharing/gig economy may involve supplies between (large) businesses, the focus of the analysis is particularly on the involvement of private individuals as this may trigger questions with respect to their treatment from a VAT/GST perspective.

Source: OECD analysis.

1.3.3. A sectoral typology based on VAT/GST relevant operational features

Sharing/gig economy activities are diverse and constantly evolving. The impact of these activities on VAT/GST policy and administration may be equally diverse and tax authorities' policy responses may need to be tailored to take account of the specific features of sharing/gig economy activity. In structuring their policy analysis and design process, it may be helpful for tax authorities to categorize the main sharing/gig economy operators and/or sectors on the basis of a set of key operational features that are likely to be relevant from a VAT/GST perspective. Figure 1.3. below suggests such sectoral typology based on sharing/gig economy activities' reliance on capital and/or labour (capital intensive vs. labour intensive) and on the mode of service delivery (digital or physical delivery). As will be discussed further in this report, these features are likely to be relevant for VAT/GST purposes, e.g. digitally delivered activities may be more likely to have cross-border aspects (could for instance be delivered remotely); capital-intensive activities may involve higher value transactions and actors that are more likely to have the capacity to comply with their tax/regulatory obligations.

Figure 1.3. A sectoral typology

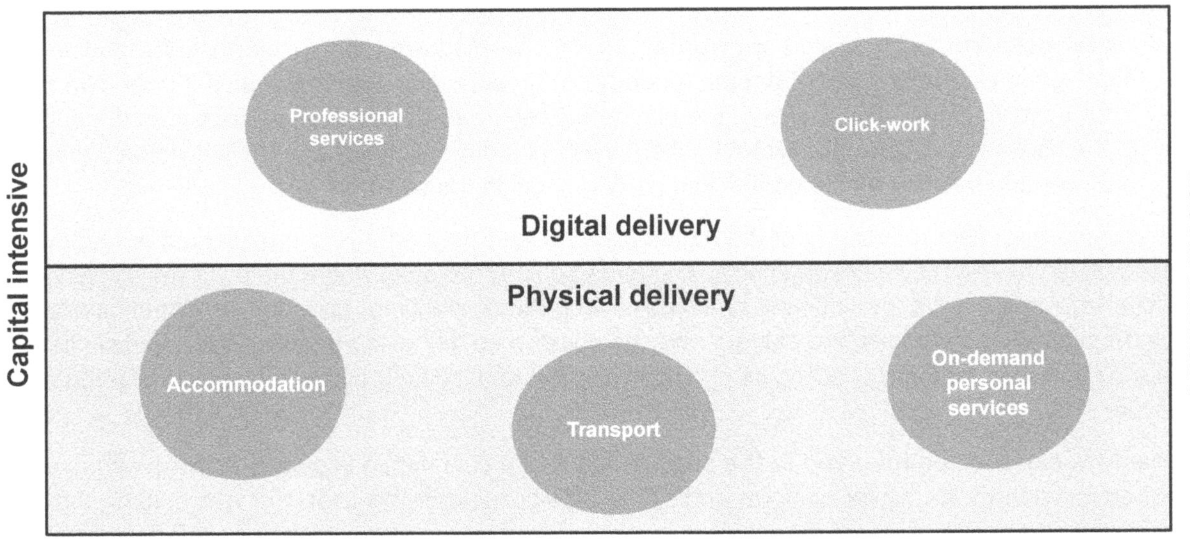

Source: OECD (2019), An Introduction to Online Platforms and their Role in the Digital Transformation (OECD, 2019[8])

1.3.4. Broad VAT/GST opportunities

The growth of the sharing/gig economy can create opportunities to facilitate and enhance VAT/GST compliance and administration and offer potential to broaden the VAT/GST base. These opportunities arise in particular from the central role of a relatively limited number of sharing/gig economy platforms in stimulating and facilitating these activities through advanced technology and data analytics. The crucial role of big data and enhanced data analysis in the sharing/gig economy business models provides considerable opportunities for greater visibility and traceability of economic activity, for formalisation of previously informal economic activity, and for more efficient tax collection and compliance.

Potential positive impact on the VAT/GST base

The sharing/gig economy is an enabler for potentially enormous numbers of individuals, often with no or limited investment, to mobilise their labour and/or assets for financial gain. The sharing/gig economy thus has the potential to expand a jurisdiction's tax base by enhancing economic activity beyond the simple substitution of an existing type of activity by a new one, by creating new markets, and/or drawing new actors in the economy. The reality is, however, more complicated. Depending on the design of a jurisdiction's VAT/GST system, the growth of the sharing/gig economy may present both an opportunity for growth and a threat to the VAT/GST base (see the section on VAT/GST challenges/risks further below).

The development of the sharing/gig economy also creates considerable opportunities to formalise activities that were not previously within reach of the VAT/GST net. One of the key drivers of the sharing/gig economy is the rapid expansion of digital connectivity via mobile devices and the strong growth of secure solutions for mobile payments. More generally, the sharing/gig economy is primarily data and technology driven. As the sharing/gig economy continues to expand and cover increasing shares and segments of economic activity, these key features are likely to create unique opportunities to reduce the cash-driven informal economy and considerably expand the formal sector, not least in developing economies.

Opportunities to increase efficiencies for tax administrations and sharing/gig economy providers

Sharing/gig economy business models and the technologies employed by the sharing/gig economy platforms are likely to provide opportunities for tax authorities to increase the efficiency of administration and collection of the tax. Beyond the opportunities for data collection and increasing the efficiency of tax collection through the involvement of the platforms (further discussed under Chapter 3), the sharing/gig economy is likely to create opportunities for tax administration to enhance the efficiency of risk-based compliance management and audit strategies, notably through systems checks at the platform level rather than carrying out audits for each individual provider. In addition, the technology-based and data-driven operation of sharing/gig economy platforms offers opportunities to significantly facilitate VAT/GST compliance for sharing/gig economy providers and to reduce these providers' compliance costs (discussed under Chapter 3). Indeed, sharing/gig economy platforms are already working closely with tax administrations in a growing number of countries to leverage these emerging opportunities (including by sharing data/information to support providers' VAT/GST compliance).

1.3.5. Broad VAT/GST challenges/risks

This section of the report discusses a number of VAT/GST challenges created or exacerbated by the growth of the sharing/gig economy. These challenges and risks may notably include the possible erosion of a jurisdiction's VAT/GST base resulting from the shift in economic activity from a relatively small number of largely tax compliant long-established traditional businesses to large numbers of new relatively small business actors (incl. non-standard workers) that may often be less compliant and/or not be subject to taxation because their activity remains below a VAT/GST exemption threshold. In addition, the varying and ever-evolving business models and types of interactions between sharing/gig economy actors may often make it particularly challenging to determine the VAT/GST nature and status of these actors and their activities and to determine and implement a proper VAT/GST treatment.

The growth of the sharing/gig economy as a (potential) threat to the VAT/GST base

Depending on the design of a jurisdiction's VAT/GST system, the growth of the sharing/gig economy may present both an opportunity for growth (discussed above) and a threat to the VAT/GST base. While VAT/GST is a broad-based consumption tax levied on most goods and services, many jurisdictions have chosen to relieve individuals and micro-businesses from the requirement to register and/or charge and account for the tax when their activities remain below a certain materiality threshold. These exemption thresholds differ from jurisdiction to jurisdiction, and differences may exist between sectors within a given jurisdiction, e.g. to minimise competitive distortion risks. In these jurisdictions, depending on the type of activity, many of the sharing/gig economy providers are likely to remain below the exemption threshold and thus be relieved from registering and/or charging VAT/GST and not contribute directly to a jurisdiction's VAT/GST revenue.

This may have an adverse effect on a jurisdiction's VAT/GST revenues, where activities carried out by traditional economic actors, which are VAT/GST registered and contribute to a jurisdiction's VAT/GST revenues, are replaced by large numbers of sharing/gig economy actors, which are below the VAT/GST registration threshold and do not contribute directly to VAT/GST revenue. This may trigger a risk of VAT/GST base erosion that may be more or less important depending on a country's economic structure and the activities involved. In the accommodation sector, for example, the sharing/gig economy may reduce the number of bookings at traditional hotels in favour of bookings with providers that are not VAT/GST registered, thus reducing the VAT/GST revenue from the hotel sector. This may increasingly create serious challenges especially for jurisdictions with a large tourism industry. Similarly, in the transportation sector, the sharing/gig economy may negatively affect the traditional taxi industry actors and reduce the VAT/GST revenue from these actors as drivers may find it easier and more flexible to switch to the sharing/gig economy activities, notably in cases where these are less regulated than their traditional counterparts.

Identifying the VAT/GST status and role of sharing/gig economy providers is not always straightforward

Identifying the VAT/GST status of the providers/users is important not only to determine economic operators' potential VAT/GST compliance obligations but also their entitlement to associated rights, in particular their right to input VAT/GST deduction.

While acknowledging that it is for a jurisdiction's national VAT/GST law to determine whether the providers of the sharing/gig economy supplies are regarded as taxable persons for VAT/GST purposes, evidence suggests that it becomes increasingly difficult to draw the line between a private individual and a taxable business for VAT/GST purposes in the sharing/gig economy. Drawing this line becomes even more challenging as in a number of cases private individuals may not (only) make use of underutilised assets/resources to develop a sharing/gig economy activity, but acquire assets with the sole purpose of exploiting them for a new economic activity (e.g. drivers purchasing cars to provide ride-sourcing services, individual owners purchasing apartment units for rental purposes only, etc.). This triggers a number of compliance and administration challenges and risks discussed further below.

Evidence suggests that many of the providers of the sharing/gig economy supplies are likely to be unknown to the VAT/GST authorities as well as be unaware of their VAT/GST obligations, or of the fact that they could benefit from simplifications to facilitate VAT/GST compliance. VAT/GST compliance risks are likely to arise from these providers' unfamiliarity with VAT/GST obligations and low level of and/or limitations to their capacity to comply. Risk analysis on the basis of data provided by sharing/gig economy platforms has confirmed these compliance risks in certain jurisdictions. These risks are likely to vary across jurisdictions and sectors, depending on a range of aspects including the VAT/GST framework (e.g. level of thresholds), its complexity, the quality of taxpayer services, compliance culture, prominent sharing/gig economy sector(s) and the profile of its providers.

Identifying the VAT/GST status of underlying providers is also an important compliance issue for sharing/gig economy platforms as it may affect their own VAT/GST obligations, including in respect of the VAT/GST treatment of fees and commissions (notably in the context of cross-border activities) and in respect of their reporting obligations (invoicing, etc.). For instance, if the transaction between the platform and the underlying sharing/gig economy provider is considered a business-to-business (B2B) supply, many jurisdictions require the VAT/GST on the commissions/fees charged by the platform to the provider to be accounted for on a reverse-charge basis when the platform is not located in the taxing jurisdiction. If the transaction is treated as business-to-consumer (B2C) supply, the platform may be required to register in the taxing jurisdiction (via a vendor registration system). To address this challenge, some platforms operate a webpage through which providers can inform the platform of their personal tax status. However, platforms often experience difficulties in verifying the underlying providers' VAT/GST registration information, notably in the absence of a reliable, real-time verification mechanism of such information operated by tax administrations.

In cases where VAT/GST registration or collection thresholds apply, the platforms may encounter additional challenges in determining whether a particular underlying provider is above or below the threshold. Particular challenges arise from the fact that underlying providers may often engage in multiple sharing/gig economy activities through multiple platforms and/or when an agent (e.g. a local booking agency) operates on a platform on behalf of multiple individual providers without making these providers' information known or visible to the platform.

The VAT/GST treatment of the sharing/gig economy activities

As illustrated in Box 1.2. above (under section 1.3.1), determining the VAT/GST treatment of sharing/gig economy activities requires the determination of the status of two main groups of interactions:

- the interactions between the sharing/gig economy platform and its users (the providers/users of the underlying activities); and
- the interactions between the sharing/gig providers and users of these activities.

In determining the VAT/GST treatment of sharing/gig economy activities, it is thus important to identify the role and status of the actors involved in the sharing/gig economy supply chain (platforms, underlying providers, users, any other third parties such as payment service providers) as well as the type of their supplies. All these aspects have an impact on the overall treatment of the supply for VAT/GST purposes, including determining the place of taxation, notably for cross-border supplies as appropriate (c.f. *International VAT/GST Guidelines* Chapter 3 (OECD, 2017[2])).

This may not always be straightforward (e.g. by simple reference to the VAT/GST treatment of similar traditional economic activities). The varying and ever-evolving business models and types of interaction(s) among the actors in the sharing/gig economy (especially, the providers and the digital platforms) have an impact on the nature of these activities and/or supplies and therefore their VAT/GST treatment.

In this context, it is critically important to determine whether the platform acts as a "principal" or as an "agent" in the sharing/gig economy supply chain, as described and illustrated in Box 1.2. under section 1.3.1. above). This determination will impact the VAT/GST treatment of the supplies involved and the associated compliance obligations for the various actors. This could include the following treatments (illustrative and non-exhaustive):

- Where a platform is considered acting as a principal, it will normally be considered as the provider of the underlying sharing/gig economy supplies to the final customers for VAT/GST purposes (e.g. transportation services). It is then for the platform to comply with all the associated VAT/GST obligations. This may notably apply where the platform acts in its own name towards the sharing/gig activity customers. This will in principle also apply where the labour model underpinning the relationship between a platform and its users has been challenged by authorities as constituting a *de facto* employer/employee relationship. Where the platform is considered acting as a principal, it may be considered as having received that same supply from the underlying sharing/gig economy provider and having supplied it onwards to the final customer. The VAT/GST treatment of this supply will notably be determined by the status of the underlying provider (including whether it acts as an independent contractor and whether its activities are above the VAT/GST exemption threshold that may be applicable in the relevant jurisdiction).
- Where the platform is considered acting as an agent, it may be considered as supplying digital/electronic services to its providers/users. The fees/commissions charged by the platform to their underlying providers/users are then treated accordingly for VAT/GST purposes, in jurisdictions where specific rules have been implemented for digital/electronic services.
- Alternatively, the services provided by the platform to its providers/users may be considered as "intermediation services", consisting of connecting sharing/gig economy providers with their customers and facilitating their interaction. These services are then treated accordingly for VAT/GST purposes.

Or

- These services may in certain cases be considered to be of the same nature with the sharing/gig economy supply by the underlying provider to the customer (e.g. considered as transportation or real estate rental services) and therefore trigger the same VAT/GST treatment.

Where cross-border supplies are involved, a different characterisation/treatment of those supplies among jurisdictions may result in cases of double and/or unintended non-taxation.

Other (third) parties can also be involved in the supply chain of a sharing/gig economy activity with direct or indirect connections to the digital platform and/or the provider and/or the final customer (end-user). This may further complicate the determination of VAT/GST treatments and obligations. For example, in the accommodation sector a real estate agent may represent a number of (individual) owners in advertising their properties on a digital platform (or multiple platforms) without these owners being known to the platform(s) (see in Annex D for an overview of other third parties that may operate in the accommodation sector).

Even within the same sharing/gig economy sector, the VAT/GST treatment of a sharing/gig supply may differ depending on the business model. This could be for instance the case for ride-sourcing for a fee and ride-sharing/car-pooling under a cost-sharing arrangement, where the determination of the consideration for the sharing/gig economy activity in a cost-sharing context (e.g. passengers pay a contribution to the estimated costs of the trip to the driver) may lead to different VAT/GST consequences. Similarly, the involvement of a consideration in-kind (e.g. in the case of exchange of houses in the accommodation sector) may create challenges notably in determining the taxable value.

Finally, as the platforms increasingly expand their offerings that may include a combination of different services/supplies (e.g. rental plus insurance) as well as non-sharing/gig economy activities either on their own or through other platforms or third parties, identifying the VAT/GST nature of these different types of (packaged or complex) services can present further challenges.

Input VAT/GST deduction challenges/risks

Sharing/gig economy providers often use assets that they also partly use for private purposes. This has great relevance for VAT/GST purposes, as input VAT/GST deduction is in principle limited to business inputs. No VAT/GST deduction is allowed for tax incurred on items used for private consumption. This raises obvious input VAT/GST deduction (and refund) risks for tax administrations, as it may be difficult to control whether many relatively small individuals have made the correct deduction. It may also raise compliance challenges for eligible providers, as it may be difficult to determine the actual amount of deductible input VAT/GST.

Tax administration and audit challenges

The rapid growth of the sharing/gig economy and the equally strong growth of self-employed sharing/gig economy workers and providers of services and assets may, over time, confront VAT/GST authorities with the challenge of dealing with large numbers of potentially new taxpayers, with a relatively small turnover and minimal knowledge of VAT/GST and other regulatory obligations and low willingness to comply. These actors may not always be visible to the tax authorities and, indeed, they may not even be located in the taxing jurisdiction.

Against the above, the tax authorities are likely to become confronted with the difficult challenge of balancing the need to protect revenue and minimise competitive distortions, which may point towards including large numbers of sharing/gig economy workers in the VAT/GST system, with the demands for an efficient tax design and administration, which may point towards limiting the number of "new" VAT/GST registrations from the sharing/gig economy, notably through high registration thresholds. This may also create pressure on tax authorities to consider alternative approaches and innovative mechanisms for the collection of tax relevant data and the VAT/GST, including through the enlistment of sharing/gig economy platforms in the VAT/GST compliance process in respect of the transactions they facilitate. Possible approaches in response to this challenge are discussed in detail under Chapter 2 and 3 of the report.

Impact on compliant operators in the traditional economy

Uncertainty around the VAT/GST treatment of sharing/gig economy actors and activities may (and is likely to) have an adverse impact on a jurisdiction's compliance culture and create competitive distortion against compliant actors in the traditional economy, notably where the sharing/gig economy actors can benefit from a price advantage caused by a *de facto* preferential VAT/GST treatment.

1.4. Overall…

This chapter has illustrated that sharing/gig economy growth can present both challenges and opportunities for VAT/GST policy and administration. It can exacerbate existing VAT/GST pressures and opportunities and/or create new ones. These pressures and opportunities are likely to differ across jurisdictions, depending on multiple factors that include the size and growth of the sharing/gig economy at national level, a jurisdiction's overall VAT/GST system, tax administration's capacity and a jurisdiction's compliance culture. Chapter 2 of this report discusses possible steps for tax authorities to consider in developing a strategy in response to the impact of the sharing/gig economy on their VAT/GST policy and administration. Chapters 3 and 4 of the report present a detailed technical discussion of the various VAT/GST policy options available to tax authorities in response to sharing/gig economy growth within their jurisdiction.

References

Constantiou, I. (2017), "Four Models of Sharing Economy Platforms", *MIS Quarterly Executive*, Vol. 16/4, https://aisel.aisnet.org/misqe/vol16/iss4/3 (accessed on 25 February 2021). [7]

Mastercard and Kaiser Associates (2019), *The Global Gig Economy: Capitalizing on a ~$500B Opportunity*, Mastercard and Kaiser Associates, https://newsroom.mastercard.com/wp-content/uploads/2019/05/Gig-Economy-White-Paper-May-2019.pdf (accessed on 25 February 2021). [5]

Nielsen (2014), *Is Sharing the New Buying?*, Nielsen, https://www.nielsen.com/wp-content/uploads/sites/3/2019/04/global-share-community-report-may-2014.pdf (accessed on 25 February 2021). [6]

OECD (2020), *Model Rules for Reporting by Platform Operators with respect to Sellers in the Sharing and Gig Economy*, OECD , Paris, https://www.oecd.org/tax/exchange-of-tax-information/model-rules-for-reporting-by-platform-operators-with-respect-to-sellers-in-the-sharing-and-gig-economy.htm (accessed on 25 February 2021). [3]

OECD (2019), *An Introduction to Online Platforms and Their Role in the Digital Transformation*, OECD Publishing, Paris, https://dx.doi.org/10.1787/53e5f593-en. [8]

OECD (2019), *The Role of Digital Platforms in the Collection of VAT/GST on Online Sales*, OECD Publishing, Paris, https://dx.doi.org/10.1787/e0e2dd2d-en. [1]

OECD (2018), *Tax Challenges Arising from Digitalisation – Interim Report 2018: Inclusive Framework on BEPS*, OECD/G20 Base Erosion and Profit Shifting Project, OECD Publishing, Paris, https://dx.doi.org/10.1787/9789264293083-en. [4]

OECD (2017), *International VAT/GST Guidelines*, OECD Publishing, Paris, https://dx.doi.org/10.1787/9789264271401-en. [2]

Notes

[1] The geographical coverage of the report focuses on Australia, Brazil, France, India, Indonesia, United Arab Emirates, United Kingdom and the United States. For the purposes of the report, the gig economy comprises of four sectors: asset-sharing (including accommodation), transportation-based services, professional services and handmade goods, household and miscellaneous services (HGHM).

[2] Sharing/gig economy activities may also involve supplies between large businesses to exploit (under)utilised capacity and generate substantial efficiency gains in respect of various input factors, primarily real capital. However, focus of the analysis is particularly on the involvement of private individuals in the sharing/gig economy supplies as this may trigger questions with respect to their treatment from a VAT/GST perspective.

2 Addressing the VAT/GST implications of the growth of the sharing/gig economy: possible steps for a needs assessment and eventual policy action

This chapter considers possible steps that a tax authority may undertake when considering its possible VAT/GST policy response to the growth of the sharing/gig economy within its jurisdiction. These steps include:

- Ensuring a good understanding of the size and growth of the sharing/gig economy at national level;
- Assessing the need (if any) for policy action and determining its key objectives (the "why" question);
- Determining and implementing the appropriate VAT/GST policy and administration response(s) (the "how" question).

Jurisdictions' VAT/GST strategies are likely to differ in light of specific facts and circumstances. They may notably not need, or wish, to go through each of these steps in developing their policy in all cases; and their responses are likely to differ in light of their specific policy needs and circumstances.

2.1. Introduction

This chapter presents a possible framework for the development of tax authorities' VAT/GST strategies in response to the growth and development of the sharing/gig economy. It recalls the various steps that tax authorities may want to take in monitoring the sharing/gig economy development and its possible impact on VAT/GST policy and administration; the needs assessment for policy action; and the determination and implementation of possible policy responses taking into account countries' specificities and circumstances. It refers to the sections of this report that provide further detailed discussion and guidance on each of these steps. This framework includes the following broad stages of policy development (see Figure 2.1. below):

Figure 2.1. Possible steps of policy development

Source: OECD analysis

The following paragraphs elaborate further on these broad stages, recognising that tax authorities may not necessarily need to go through all of them as their responses are likely to differ depending on national circumstances and policy objectives.

2.2. Ensuring a good understanding of the size and growth of the sharing/gig economy at national level

To support evidence-based decision making, jurisdictions considering the potential need for VAT/GST action in response to the sharing/gig economy development are likely to need a proper and up-to-date understanding of the size and growth perspectives of this economy at national level. Chapter 1 of this report presents an analysis of the sharing/gig economy, its main actors and sectors, their growth perspectives and the business models they operate. This is aimed at supporting tax authorities in deepening their understanding of the sharing/gig economy within their jurisdiction and in organising their further monitoring of this economy's development.

Monitoring the sharing/gig economy in further detail is challenging, notably due to the often informal nature of the activities of sharing/gig economy participants, which may often be unregistered or underreport for tax purposes, and due to difficulties related to the classification of activities. National accounts procedures tend to reflect conditions before the emergence of the sharing/gig economy, notably for informal rental and labour activity. Similarly, even though household surveys help to measure the labour activity, respondents often neglect to report gig activities unless explicitly asked about the topic in questionnaires (IMF, 2018[1]) (OECD, 2019[2]).

Monitoring and measuring the sharing/gig economy obviously has a relevance beyond VAT/GST policy. It is therefore beyond the scope of this report to discuss this aspect of government policy in respect of the sharing/gig economy in any particular detail. It would seem obvious, however, as a general consideration, that jurisdictions adopt a coordinated, whole-of-government approach in monitoring and measuring the sharing/gig economy to support a consistent, fact-based, and effective and targeted policy strategy and implementation.

To this end jurisdictions may wish to develop a framework to define and collect statistical data on the sharing/gig economy activities. Imposing data reporting obligations on actors involved in the sharing/gig economy supply chain, notably the digital platforms facilitating those sharing/gig economy supplies (further discussed under Chapter 3 of the report) could allow jurisdictions to make quick progress in improving the measurement of the sharing/gig economy and therefore acquire a better understanding of its size and growth at national level. Of particular relevance in this context is the 2019 OECD report on *Measuring platform mediated workers* as part of the OECD Digital Economy Papers series by the OECD Directorate for Science, Technology and Innovation (STI) (OECD, 2019[2]). While recognising challenges in estimating the number of platform workers, this report reviews different attempts by private agencies and official statistical agencies to measure platform workers and offers recommendations on how to improve the measurement in the future (i.e. how to use different forms of surveys / how to formulate the survey questions to obtain desired outcomes).

2.3. Assessing the need (if any) for policy action and determining its key objectives (addressing the "why" question)

The main motivation for possible VAT/GST policy action in response to sharing/gig economy developments is likely to differ across jurisdictions, but will generally relate to securing revenues and addressing risks of competitive distortion. The main drivers for possible VAT/GST measures are likely to include the size and growth of the sharing/gig economy or specific sectors of this economy in a given jurisdiction, the pressure it creates on the VAT/GST base and revenues, and on the competitive position of the economically equivalent traditional sectors.

VAT/GST pressures caused by sharing/gig economy growth will vary depending on the economic sector(s) involved and on the specific features of jurisdictions' VAT/GST design, such as the presence and level of registration and/or collection thresholds. Sharing/gig economy growth typically involves growing activity by potentially large numbers of new economic actors and/or non-standard workers that may qualify as VAT/GST taxpayers under existing rules. In a jurisdiction with a relatively high VAT/GST registration or collection threshold, which applies to all economic activity or specifically to the sector in which the sharing/gig economy growth occurs, this sharing/gig economy growth is likely to cause VAT/GST pressures of a different nature than in a jurisdiction with no or a low VAT/GST threshold. In a jurisdiction with a high threshold, the revenue and competitive impacts of new sharing/gig economy actors (e.g. occasional gig workers) entering a given market sector may be limited as the existing traditional economy actors in that sector may generally be below the threshold as well. On the other hand, revenue and competitive consequences may be significant when sharing/gig economy growth results in activity shifting from a relatively small number of large traditional operators that are above the VAT/GST threshold to a large number of small sharing/gig economy operators that are generally below the threshold given its relatively high level (e.g. hotel activity vs. short-term vacation rentals). In a jurisdiction with no or low threshold, the growth of the sharing/gig economy sector(s) may create pressure on tax administration as a large number of small businesses may enter the VAT/GST system, perhaps with limited compliance capacity and knowledge of their tax obligations.

A jurisdiction's main objective may not necessarily be to bring all sharing/gig economy activities within the VAT/GST net. A jurisdiction may for instance wish to start by monitoring sharing/gig economy development to ensure a proper assessment of any potential risk of VAT/GST base erosion and/or competitive distortions so as to allow rapid and targeted policy action when considered appropriate. The choice of the most appropriate VAT/GST measures in response to sharing/gig economy growth and the design of these measures is heavily dependent on the policy objectives that tax authorities wish to pursue through their policy action. Chapter 1 discussed the main pressures that sharing/gig economy growth may cause for VAT/GST policy and administration. In response to these pressures, Figure 2.2. below recalls the main motivations for VAT/GST policy action.

Figure 2.2. Addressing the VAT/GST implications of the sharing/gig economy – Often (a mix of) diverse key policy objectives in practice

Source: OECD analysis

Given the diversity of the sharing/gig economy landscape and its constantly evolving nature, jurisdictions' need for policy action and its objectives are likely to vary depending on the sectors of the sharing/gig economy that are active in their domestic market, on their relative size and growth and on their impact on existing economic activity. Depending on the outcome of their assessment of sharing/gig economy developments within their jurisdiction, tax authorities may opt for a sequenced strategy focusing their policy action first on the dominant sharing/gig economy sectors that may create the most immediate risks to VAT/GST revenue and/or competitive neutrality (e.g. ride-sourcing, short-term rentals), while continuing to monitor the other (emerging) sectors to ensure early identification of further needs for policy action.

A clear understanding of the objective(s) of VAT/GST policy action in response to sharing/gig economy developments in a given jurisdiction is critical for identifying the most appropriate policy response and for determining the design of this response. If the objective is to purely monitor sharing/gig economy developments, then the introduction of data reporting requirements on platforms and other sharing/gig economy actors is likely to be part of the policy response. However, such a reporting requirements could also be aimed at supporting VAT/GST collection and compliance, for instance, by pre-populating VAT/GST returns of gig economy workers, or to detect non-compliance and/or support compliance through risk analysis.

2.4. Determining and implementing the appropriate VAT/GST policy and administration response (addressing the "how" question)

There is no one-size-fits-all solution for addressing the VAT/GST implications associated with the growth of the sharing/gig economy. A tax authority's policy response to sharing/gig economy developments in a given jurisdiction will depend heavily on the various possible motivations for its policy action, as outlined above, which will in their turn be dependent on the specific aspects of the sharing/gig economy activity in that jurisdiction and their impact on VAT/GST revenues and on the competitive position of traditional economic activity.

The design and implementation of measures can therefore be expected to reflect the differences in policy and legislative environments, tax authorities' distinct challenges and priorities and the diversity of sharing/gig economy business models. It is for individual jurisdictions to determine which measures are most appropriate for their particular circumstances. This report aims at assisting jurisdictions by analysing the main available policy and administration options and identifying a number of aspects that jurisdictions may wish to take into account. These options are discussed in detail in Chapter 3 of this report. The remaining paragraphs of this Chapter 2 discuss a number of overarching policy aspects and design principles for jurisdictions to consider in their policy decision process.

2.4.1. Is there a need to review normal VAT/GST rules in response to sharing/gig economy developments?

There may be no good reason or justification, in principle, for a different VAT/GST treatment of sharing/gig economy activities compared to similar or identical activities in the traditional or broader platform economy, only because sharing/gig economy activities are facilitated via a different (digital) channel. This observation is not only based on competitive neutrality principles but also on the findings of this report suggesting that sharing/gig economy activities and sectors are increasingly merging with traditional and other digital activities and sectors (e.g. traditional actors and or e-commerce marketplaces creating their own sharing/gig economy platforms or connecting with existing ones). A sharing/gig economy-specific policy response introducing specific measures that deviate from normal VAT/GST rules may then not be the most appropriate response, as it may cause undue complexity and require continuous updating. On the other hand, bringing the sharing/gig economy within the application of normal VAT/GST rules, may require adjustments to these rules to address the specific challenges that the specific features of this economy may create for VAT/GST policy and administration.

Whether a jurisdiction decides to opt for the adoption of broader changes to its VAT/GST system or for more targeted measures will notably depend on the jurisdiction's VAT/GST system and the pressures that the sharing/gig economy growth creates for VAT/GST policy and administration. In a jurisdiction with no or a low registration threshold, for instance, the growth of the sharing/gig economy may create the pressure of having to administer large numbers of new economic actors entering the VAT/GST system, perhaps with limited capacity and knowledge of their tax obligations. This may lead to a need to review this jurisdiction's threshold policy accordingly and/or consider other alternative approaches to facilitate compliance and VAT/GST collection, e.g. involving digital platforms, presumptive schemes, etc.

Against this background, the natural starting point for jurisdictions in considering VAT/GST policy responses to the sharing/gig economy is to test the application of the existing VAT/GST framework

against the specifics of the sharing/gig economy and to consider responses that are consistent with this framework to address any specific challenges where appropriate. Such an approach will serve to avoid overlapping or conflicting obligations that may result from specific measures that may diverge from the existing VAT/GST framework, which could lead to additional complexity and uncertainty and more compliance burdens and administration costs. In other words, jurisdictions may first need to identify any policy and administration gaps in their current VAT/GST framework before being able to determine what type of policy action may be required to address any VAT/GST challenges created by the sharing/gig economy.

Similarly, jurisdictions may also need to consider the potential interaction of their current VAT/GST system with other areas of national law, including labour law, social security legislation and/or the income tax regime. For instance, the treatment of a sharing/gig economy platform as an employer and the underlying providers as employees under a jurisdiction's labour law, may have an impact on the VAT/GST treatment of this activity. Similarly, the requirement for a VAT/GST registration as a condition to obtain a license to carry out an activity or to take on a certain job, or to be eligible for social security coverage or for specific allowances may influence the VAT/GST response.

2.4.2. Is there a need for sector-specific policies in the sharing/gig economy?

Related to the previous discussion is the question whether or to what extent different policy responses may be appropriate depending on the specific sector of the sharing/gig economy involved. The diversity of sharing/gig economy activities (e.g. asset-based vs. labour-based) and business models (e.g. electronic/web-based payment vs. cash-based payment) can lead to an equally diverse set of compliance and/or administration challenges that may justify a differentiation of policy responses.

In line with what was highlighted before, where a differentiated approach may be considered appropriate, it is advisable to opt for a policy response that is consistent with the general rules and principles of the jurisdiction's VAT/GST system and to limit the introduction of new exceptions or special regimes. The introduction of specific regimes targeting specific sectors, e.g. through sector-specific thresholds or exemptions, may create additional complexity and uncertainty notably as the constantly evolving nature of sharing/gig economy sectors and their convergence across sectors (which notably results in bundled offerings) may make it exceedingly difficult to delineate the application of these regimes. This may lead to increased compliance burdens and risks of competitive distortion and non-compliance (e.g. from mischaracterisation of activities to benefit from the most attractive VAT/GST treatment). A sector-specific approach may also be less future proof in light of the continuous changes to business models and emergence of new sharing/gig economy sectors quickly gaining significance.

It is recognised that a differentiated policy response may effectively be required and be appropriate in light of the specific features of specific sharing/gig economy sectors. For instance, an effective policy response to the emergence of a sector/gig economy activity that relies on the physical presence of the underlying service providers (e.g. short-distance transport services) could be different than the policy response to an activity that involves the provision of remote services from abroad (e.g. intellectual gig work) or that relies on the presence of assets in a jurisdiction that may be foreign-owned (e.g. real-estate rental). Overall, a response that is embedded in and consistent with the overall VAT/GST framework is likely to be the most effective.

It is recognised that a jurisdiction may decide to adopt gradual policy action. In particular, it may decide to first target dominant sharing/gig economy sectors that create the most pressing VAT/GST revenue risks and/or concerns of competitive distortion. In this context, a jurisdiction may consider running a (voluntary) pilot programme with actors in these sectors, and then further rolling out this across these sectors building on the experience of the pilot programme. Equally, the know-how and experience acquired in implementing a reform targeted at sharing/gig economy sectors that were identified as needing a priority response, are likely to serve as a good basis for further policy action in response to developments in other sharing/gig economy sectors.

Broadening the scope of existing policies to cover other types of sharing/gig economy activities will need to be carefully designed so as to ensure the workability of such policies in light of the diversity of sharing/gig economy business models. This is for example the case when considering broadening the scope of data/sharing reporting obligations for actors in specific sectors to other sharing/gig economy sectors and actors. Determining the reportable information elements on the basis of available information per sector is of particular relevance to ensure an efficient and effective operation of such a regime (see further Annex D that illustrates variations of business models operating even within the same sector and information elements available to the platforms depending on the type of their operations).

2.4.3. Overarching design principles for tax policy and administration approaches to address the VAT/GST implications of the sharing/gig economy.

In principle, an effective VAT/GST system is a system in which policy objectives, legislation, administration, compliance strategies and taxpayer services are carefully aligned. A response that is properly grounded in the overall VAT/GST framework and that is consistent with its overall operation is most likely to deliver on revenue and equity objectives, on compliance efficiency for sharing/gig economy actors and on administrative effectiveness for the tax authorities. A well-balanced response will also prevent that VAT/GST policy create undue impediments to sharing/gig economy development. The *Ottawa Taxation Framework Conditions* may provide useful guidance in designing such reform, building on the fundamental principles of Neutrality, Efficiency, Certainty and Simplicity, Effectiveness and Fairness and Flexibility.

To conclude, and recognising that there is no such thing as a "one-size-fits-all solution", this chapter outlines a number of additional overarching VAT/GST policy design principles to further inform tax authorities' analysis and decision in response to sharing/gig economy developments within their jurisdiction:

- **Reach a clear understanding of the intended policy objectives** and evaluate potential strategy/policy options against these objectives.
- **Ensure equal treatment of various distribution channels in a given market, be they traditional or digital,** while accepting that policy action may be needed to achieve such equal treatment for sharing/gig economy activities in light of the specific features of this economy. As the platform economy, including the sharing/gig economy, converges with the wider economy it is essential that channel neutrality is safeguarded between providers operating via platforms and those operating offline.
- **Build the design of policy options on a good understanding of the sharing/gig economy actors, their ecosystems and trends so as to ensure their workability in a proportionate and future proof manner**. Hence, the importance of tax administrations consulting with the stakeholders involved (i.e. sharing/gig economy actors; traditional economic operators and other third-party stakeholders such as service and IT providers).
- **Ensure close co-operation with other government agencies** (e.g. labour regulators) to explore opportunities for whole-of-government approaches. These could include providing cross-agency access to VAT/GST relevant information collected by other (non-VAT/GST) national agencies and vice versa; as well as a "one-stop-shop" registration process covering several purposes and governmental agencies/entities/authorities.
- **Participate in international dialogue with peers in other jurisdictions** to stay informed of global trends and share analysis, experience and best practices. The Global Forum on VAT and the Forum on Tax Administration can play a useful role in facilitating such dialogue.

- **Ensure proper communication of policy measures in advance of their introduction** – and provide adequate lead-time for their implementation along with clear guidance for all the sharing/gig economy actors involved (providers, users and platforms).
- **Safeguard the integrity of the tax system by facilitating compliance and keeping compliance burdens proportionate while mitigating risks of tax evasion and avoidance.** To this end, tax authorities are encouraged to adopt a two-pronged approach, whereby, on the one hand compliance is facilitated and encouraged by simplifying procedures and on the other hand creating a deterrent for non-compliance.
- **Evaluate on a regular basis the efficiency/neutrality of policies adopted including their (potential) impact on the growth of the sharing/gig economy.** Sharing/gig economy is an evolving area. Developments including in the regulatory domain (e.g. labour law related developments that could reshape the relations between the platforms and their provider) and technological landscape (e.g. the potential use of self-driving cars in the future) could transform the scope and scale of the sharing/gig economy rapidly both at national and global level. Hence there is a need to monitor developments and evaluate the efficiency/neutrality of policies adopted at -to the extent possible- regular intervals.

These overarching design principles serve as the evaluation framework for assessing the efficiency and effectiveness of a wide range of policy and administration options including also potential roles for digital platforms further considered under Chapter 3 of the report.

References

IMF (2018), "Measuring the Digital Economy", *Policy Papers*, IMF , Washington, D.C., https://www.imf.org/en/Publications/Policy-Papers/Issues/2018/04/03/022818-measuring-the-digital-economy (accessed on 25 February 2021). [1]

OECD (2019), "Measuring platform mediated workers", *OECD Digital Economy Papers*, No. 282, OECD Publishing, Paris, https://dx.doi.org/10.1787/170a14d9-en. [2]

3 Addressing the VAT/GST implications of the sharing/gig economy growth: A range of tax policy and administration options - The role of digital platforms

This chapter of the report analyses a range of potential VAT/GST policy and administration options that jurisdictions may wish to consider in designing their strategy to address the potential VAT/GST pressures created by the growth of the sharing/gig economy.

In particular, it considers a range of non-mutually exclusive tax and administrative measures to facilitate and enhance VAT/GST compliance in the sharing/gig economy, in particular through the simplification of VAT/GST compliance processes, the collection and effective use of data and (alternative) approaches for the collection of the VAT/GST due on sharing/gig economy supplies (in Section 3.2). This is complemented with a detailed analysis of the potential roles of digital sharing/gig economy platforms in facilitating and enhancing VAT/GST compliance in the sharing/gig economy (in Section 3.3). While recognising that there is no one-size-fits-all solution, the key objective is to discuss associated policy considerations (opportunities and challenges) and assist policy makers in their efforts to evaluate and develop the legal and administrative framework in their jurisdictions taking into account their own national circumstances and key policy motivations.

3.1. Introduction

As discussed under Chapter 2, the key policy motivations for the development of a VAT/GST strategy in response to sharing/gig economy growth are likely to differ across jurisdictions. These will depend on a number of factors, including the size and growth of (a sector of) the sharing/gig economy in a given jurisdiction, its possible impact on the VAT/GST base and revenues, and the competitive pressure it creates for the economic equivalent sector(s). It is recognised that a jurisdiction's policy priority may not necessarily involve the levying of VAT/GST on all sharing/gig economy activities but may for instance be aimed at addressing the need to acquire an appropriate understanding of the sharing/gig economy development and to monitor any potential risk of VAT/GST base erosion so as to inform future policy decisions as appropriate.

Given the diversity of policy motivations and challenges for jurisdictions, there is no one-size-fits-all response to the VAT/GST implications of the sharing/gig economy. It is reasonable to expect that the design and implementation of potential measures will reflect the differences in policy and legislative environments, tax authorities' distinct challenges and key policy objectives and the diversity of sharing/gig economy business models. It is for individual jurisdictions to determine which measures are most appropriate for their particular circumstances. The key objective of this report is to identify potential options and discuss associated policy considerations (opportunities and challenges) to assist policy makers in evaluating and developing their policy and administrative response taking into account their national specificities.

This report recognises that the VAT/GST status of the sharing/gig economy actors (including platforms and underlying providers) in a given jurisdiction will generally be determined on the basis of that jurisdiction's normal VAT/GST rules, often on a case-by-case basis in light of specific facts and circumstances. This includes the question whether a sharing/gig economy platform acts as a principal or as an agent for VAT/GST purposes. Indeed, as set out in Chapter 1, the activities carried out in the sharing/gig economy are generally not new and they are in principle captured by normal VAT/GST rules. It is the use of technology to facilitate and deliver these activities that is new and that creates challenges and opportunities for VAT/GST policy and administration, as sharing/gig economy platforms generate and stimulate the activity of potentially large numbers of new economic actors that may become subject to VAT/GST under normal rules. This new commercial reality may create considerable pressure for VAT/GST administration, as it may notably bring large numbers of private individuals into the VAT/GST system with limited VAT/GST knowledge and/or capacity to comply (i.e. micro-businesses, SMEs), whose activities may be hard to track and involve VAT/GST revenues and competitive distortions that are limited on an individual level but that may be significant at an aggregated level. The aim of this Chapter is to present a range of possible options for tax policy and administration to address these challenges.

It is recognised that the tax authorities may face the difficult challenge of balancing the need to protect revenue and minimise competitive distortions, which may point towards bringing large numbers of new and relatively small economic actors into the VAT/GST system, with the need to safeguard the efficiency of tax administration and to avoid undue compliance burden for sharing/gig economy actors. This may often be a complex exercise that requires careful consideration of a range of different parameters, including the national policy context and the specifics of a given sharing/gig economy activity or sector.

Against this background, this chapter considers a range of non-mutually exclusive policy and administration measures for the efficient application of VAT/GST to the sharing/gig economy. These include possible options to simplify VAT/GST administration and compliance as well as approaches for the efficient and effective collection of tax relevant data and for the collection of the VAT/GST due on sharing/gig economy supplies.

These measures can be grouped in two broad categories as illustrated in Figure 3.1.:

Figure 3.1. A wide range of policy options

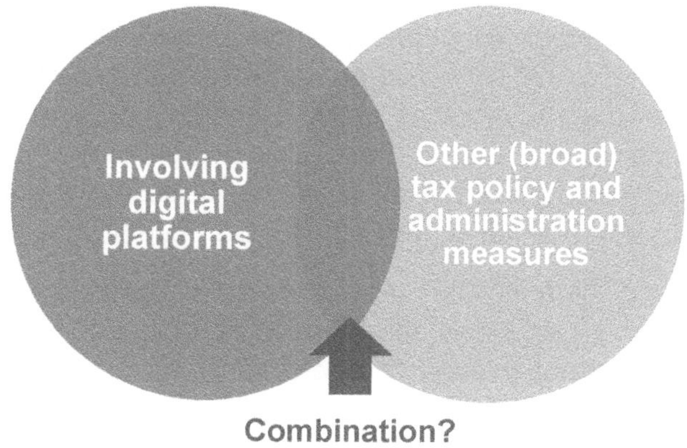

No one-size-fits-all solution

A hybrid/incremental approach could be a possible answer

In light of specific sector/business model + policy objective + national circumstances

Source: OECD analysis.

- **Broad VAT/GST policy and administration measures,** which are available for potential application to both traditional activities and similar sharing/gig economy activities. These present a range of possible measures for tax authorities to implement an equal treatment of traditional and corresponding sharing/gig economy sectors, while minimising risks of undue administrative burdens and compliance costs. These measures essentially aim at managing the number of new economic actors entering the VAT/GST system, and at simplifying compliance obligations for sharing/gig economy providers, notably by using the opportunities offered by technology to facilitate reporting and VAT/GST collection. These options are further analysed under Section 3.2. and include:
  - Determination of the VAT/GST registration and/or collection threshold;
  - Presumptive schemes for determining the VAT/GST liability;
  - Accounting and reporting simplifications;
  - Implementation of split payment/withholding mechanisms for VAT/GST collection;
  - Using technology to support VAT/GST administration and facilitate compliance;
  - Introduce third-party reporting obligations;
  - Taxpayer education and other awareness raising activities.

- **Measures focused specifically on digital platforms in light of their prominent role in generating and facilitating sharing/gig economy activities:**
  - Educating the underlying suppliers on their VAT/GST obligations;
  - Providing data to the tax authorities, so as to allow these authorities to monitor the sharing/gig economy, to facilitate compliance and administration and/or to manage compliance risks;
  - Collecting the VAT/GST and/or assuming a type of liability for the VAT/GST on the sharing/gig economy supplies that they facilitate.

These measures on possible roles for sharing/gig economy platforms are further considered under Section 3.3. This section relates exclusively to platforms that facilitate supplies by sharing/gig economy providers to their customers, but which do not have the obligation to report or pay the VAT/GST on these supplies under normal VAT/GST rules (i.e. they act under the agent role). They do not relate to sharing/gig economy platforms that already have the obligations to report and/or remit the VAT/GST on sharing/gig economy supplies, notably as a consequence of their treatment as the VAT/GST supplier of these supplies under normal rules. They also do no relate to the normal VAT/GST obligations for digital platform in respect of the commissions or fees that they collect for their activities from the sharing/gig economy provider or the user or both. This section builds further on the 2019 Digital Platforms report, highlighting the possible differences in the operation of sharing/gig economy platforms and their impact on their possible roles in supporting VAT/GST compliance (OECD, 2019[1]).

As discussed under Chapter 2, there may be no good reason or justification, in principle, for a different VAT/GST treatment of sharing/gig economy activities compared to similar or identical activities in the traditional or broader platform economy, only because sharing/gig economy activities are facilitated via a different (digital) channel. The application of normal VAT/GST rules and compliance obligations for both sharing/gig economy providers and suppliers operating under similar circumstances in the traditional economy or in other sectors of the platform economy, will normally achieve competitive neutrality from a VAT/GST perspective.

It is recognised, however, that jurisdictions may wish to consider specific measures tailored to the specific features of the sharing/gig economy (e.g. the availability of technology to support compliance) or to achieve broader policy objectives (e.g. monitoring sector developments), which could ultimately result in a different tax treatment. In practice, in designing their sharing/gig economy policies, tax authorities may need to consider the appropriate trade-off between the objective to enhance compliance and revenue collection in the sharing/gig economy and the possible differences in the VAT/GST treatment of sharing/gig economy operators that may result from these policies (e.g. as a consequence of the application of a presumptive scheme). Identifying the appropriate rationale for differences in VAT/GST treatment, where appropriate, is an inevitably challenging task for tax authorities.[1] To safeguard the overall integrity of their VAT/GST system, tax authorities are generally advised to minimise complexity and administrative burdens and compliance costs that may result from specific VAT/GST rules for the sharing/gig economy and to minimise their vulnerability to non-compliance and evasion.

Chapter 4 of the report discusses a number of risk-based compliance and enforcement approaches for tax administrations to consider in ensuring appropriate levels of compliance with the measures considered in Chapter 3.

3.2. Broader tax policy options

This section considers a number of broader tax policy and administration options that essentially aim at managing the number of new economic actors entering the VAT/GST system, and at simplifying compliance obligations for sharing/gig economy providers, notably by using the opportunities offered by technology to facilitate reporting and VAT/GST collection. The relevant analysis builds on the recognition that the VAT/GST status of the sharing/gig economy providers and other actors in a given jurisdiction will generally be determined on the basis of that jurisdiction's normal VAT/GST rules, often on a case-by-case basis in light of specific facts and circumstances.

3.2.1. The application of registration and/or collection thresholds

Many VAT/GST regimes apply one or multiple thresholds typically aimed at small businesses below which such a business is relieved from the obligation to charge and remit VAT/GST on its outputs and from the associated reporting obligations. These thresholds are generally based on annual turnover. Broadly two categories can be distinguished: registration thresholds that relieve a business from both the requirement to register and to collect the VAT/GST; and collection thresholds where a business is required to register for VAT/GST, even when their turnover is below the threshold, but is relieved from collecting the VAT/GST until it exceeds the threshold. Thresholds may vary according to sector or type of activity and sector.

The impact of sharing/gig economy growth on VAT/GST policy and administration, including on revenues and competitive neutrality, is likely to depend on a VAT/GST system's threshold policy:

- *a jurisdiction with a relatively high VAT/GST registration or collection threshold* (in general or sector-specific) may in particular be faced with VAT/GST base erosion and revenue losses in sectors where sharing/gig economy growth leads to a shift of activity from a relative small number of economic operators that are above the threshold (e.g. hotels) to a multitude of relatively small and new economic operators (e.g. owners of real estate that is offered for short-term rental) that are below the threshold. This may lead to rapidly increasing revenue losses and market distortions, including operators organising themselves to keep their activities below the threshold so as to remain competitive.
- *a jurisdiction with no or a low VAT/GST threshold,* may face the administrative challenge of large numbers of small and new economic operators entering the VAT/GST system as the consequence of sharing/gig economy growth, often with a limited capacity to understand and comply with their VAT/GST obligations (e.g. gig workers). This may also increase the number of taxpayers entitled to input VAT/GST deduction (e.g. VAT/GST incurred on fuel costs by drivers in the transportation sector) with a correspondingly high administrative burden and potential revenue risks, as the assets used (e.g. cars or houses) will often be used also for private purposes.

Thresholds can thus be a useful tool for jurisdictions in managing the impact of sharing/gig economy growth on VAT/GST revenues and administration. A high threshold may reduce the pressure on the VAT/GST administration from large numbers of new small businesses entering the system with costs and compliance risks that may be disproportionate to the VAT/GST revenues raised. For sharing/gig economy providers, it avoids VAT/GST compliance costs that could often be disproportionate to their turnover. A relatively low threshold can limit risks of base erosion and competitive distortion and act as an incentive for businesses to formalise their activity. Designing this tool will thus be a delicate balancing act. There is no one-size-fits-all answer to what constitutes a "good" level for the VAT/GST threshold. A number of factors need to be considered by a jurisdiction when setting the level of threshold. The level of the threshold will typically be the result of a trade-off between minimising compliance and administration costs, and the need to protect revenue and avoid competitive distortion.

When considering the use of VAT/GST thresholds as a tool to manage the VAT/GST impact of sharing/gig economy growth, the following factors may be considered:

- the core features of the relevant sharing/gig economy sector, particularly its size and growth perspective and the typical profile of the (new) economic operators that will become active as sharing/gig economy providers. The answer to these questions may help to indicate whether the revenue risks and the risks of competitive distortion are considered sufficiently important to warrant policy action – and to what extent a shift of activity from traditional economy operators to sharing/gig economy operators can lead to such loss of revenue and competitive distortion and to increased pressure on tax administration. The outcome of this analysis may for instance be different for a sector that is labour-intensive and requires limited financial investment (e.g. "gig-work"), than for a sector that is more capital intensive (e.g. short-term rental). The former may attract high numbers of new economic operators with perhaps less capacity to comply with VAT/GST requirements and challenging for tax administrations to track. The latter may be less numerous and relatively easier to track, and could be presumed to have a higher capability to comply with their tax obligations;

- the complexity of the VAT/GST regime and compliance obligations and the associated compliance costs for sharing/gig economy operators;
- the availability of a simplified accounting and reporting regime for small businesses, including a simplified regime for calculating VAT/GST liability. The availability of such simplification measures could for instance justify a relatively low threshold for a given sharing/gig economy sector;
- the capacity of the tax administration to manage and monitor a large(r) number of VAT/GST-registered taxpayers, including the administration costs connected with tax supervision and collection;
- the tax morale in the population of (small) businesses.

It is thus obviously a matter for each jurisdiction to determine the level of the threshold depending on its circumstances, with potential trade-offs between encouraging new economic activity and reduction of the cash/informal economy, and potentially impacting competition in particular sectors. In this context, the following aspects would merit further consideration by interested jurisdictions:

- Consider the availability of a voluntary registration scheme for small businesses, including sharing/gig economy actors, who may be disadvantaged by the VAT/GST exemption. That may notably apply to businesses that wish to recover the VAT/GST on their inputs and/or that deal with VAT/GST registered customers who themselves only wish to contract with VAT/GST registered providers to avoid VAT/GST cascading (such cascading can result for unregistered providers passing on the cost of irrecoverable VAT/GST to their customers). The option for voluntary registration may also stimulate and accommodate business to organise their business with a view of soon exceeding the threshold (and who therefore immediately design their processes with VAT/GST). Such voluntary registration could be allowed under the condition that the business remains registered for a minimum period of time so as to avoid VAT/GST fraud by "fly-by-night" providers who may register and ask for refund claims on an *ad hoc* basis;
- Consider the implementation of anti-abuse measures, e.g. to counter sharing/gig economy operators artificially dividing their activities among a number of sharing/gig economy platforms or other distribution channels to stay below the threshold. Such measures could include collecting and cross-checking data from digital platforms and leveraging on technology enabled solutions (see analysis below).

The annual turnover is often the basis for determining a VAT/GST threshold. However, a jurisdiction may wish to differentiate the determination of a VAT/GST threshold depending on the sector and by reference to (additional) indicators that are typical and considered relevant for a given activity. In the accommodation sector, for instance, such an indicator could include the type of property that is offered for short-term rental (e.g. room in the principal residency vs. an entire apartment). In the transportation sector, the number of journeys per specific period (month/year) could be considered as an additional indicator. It is recognised though that this type of activity indicators per sector could increase complexity and make administration and compliance more challenging.

A threshold can be used as a tool allowing tax authority to decide how far they wish to "cast the net" to bring sharing/gig economy operators within the VAT/GST system and/or exclude from it.[2] Where a jurisdiction opts to bring (a part of) sharing/gig economy providers within the VAT/GST system via a (lower) threshold, it may need to consider options for simplifying VAT/GST compliance for small businesses including for a simple determination of VAT/GST liability and/or payment of the VAT/GST due. Possible policy options for such simplification and for enhancing the efficiency of VAT/GST administration and compliance more generally are discussed in the following sections of this chapter.

3.2.2. Presumptive VAT/GST schemes

Presumptive VAT/GST schemes can be particularly helpful in reducing VAT/GST compliance burden for the eligible (small) businesses and thus allow for sharing/gig economy actors to be brought into the VAT/GST system without creating undue compliance cost and complexity. A core relevant feature of presumptive schemes is that they typically simplify the accounting and calculation of VAT/GST liability by notably removing the need to determine the recoverability of VAT/GST on individual expense items. This can lead to significant simplification for the application of VAT/GST for sharing/gig economy activities, which often involve assets that are used for both business and private purposes (e.g., vehicles, real-estate). This may often create challenges for sharing/gig economy providers to determine the correct amount of deductible input VAT/GST, and for tax administration to police the correct deduction of VAT/GST by large numbers of relatively small business operators.

The main relevant variations of presumptive VAT/GST schemes may include:

- **A simplified input tax credit calculation scheme,** under which eligible taxpayers must charge VAT/GST on their outputs in line with regular VAT/GST provisions but are granted a fixed input VAT/GST deduction from the amount of VAT/GST due. Hence, the amount of VAT/GST to be paid to tax authorities is calculated differently than under normal rules (which require the amount of VAT/GST that has actually been incurred on business inputs to be offset against the output VAT). Such an approach reduces the VAT/GST compliance burden for eligible taxpayers, as it removes the need to determine the recoverability of VAT/GST on individual expense items. Under a simplified input tax credit calculation scheme, setting the level of the fixed input tax deduction requires careful consideration so as to avoid any unintended consequences, e.g., an inappropriately high level resulting in a subsidy for eligible taxpayers and eventual distortion of competition. The level of fixed input-VAT/GST deduction will typically need to be established on the basis of sector analysis (sector averages). This challenge may be less important in a labour-intensive sector where the amounts of deductible input VAT/GST may be smaller. Where a business typically supplies to other VAT/GST registered businesses, which have a right to the full deduction of input VAT/GST, tax authorities will need to consider to what extent the application of the simplified input tax credit calculation scheme has undue revenue consequences given that the overall amount of VAT/GST deducted may not correspond with the amount of VAT/GST that has been remitted to the tax authorities.
- **Application of a specific VAT/GST rate (a "flat-rate") on the outputs of the eligible taxpayers,** taking into account the taxpayer's presumed (average) right to input VAT/GST deduction. Under such a regime, eligible taxpayers charge VAT/GST at a specific (lower than the normal) rate but will not have any right to input VAT/GST deduction. The flat rates for determining the VAT/GST liability under such a presumptive scheme are intended to reflect the average effective VAT/GST rate in the relevant sector in light of the average estimated recovery of VAT/GST on inputs in that sector. The variation of applicable flat rates will notably be relevant in the sharing/gig economy where labour-intensive activities may typically incur less input VAT/GST than capital-intensive (asset-based) sectors which could potentially justify the application of different flat rates. The determination of these flat rates requires a good understanding of the ecosystem in which those sharing/gig economy actors operate and therefore a close consultation with the stakeholders involved. However, it is recognised that the variation of flat tax rates among different sectors of sharing/gig economy could create distortions and policing problems in cases where a sharing/gig economy provider is involved in multiple activities that may be subject to different flat rates.
- **A lump-sum scheme** under which the eligible taxpayer's VAT/GST liability is determined on a lump-sum basis instead of through the normal process based on the taxpayer's actual supplies. This lump-sum is based solely on a number of specific indicators per type of supply, e.g., type of properties provided for short-term leasing, the number of journeys performed, etc.

- **Application of a VAT/GST input tax credit/recovery scheme through the provider's income tax return.** Under such a scheme the taxpayer charges the normal VAT/GST rate on its supplies but any input VAT credit/recovery is calculated on the basis of (grossed up) income tax expenses claimed by the taxpayer via its income tax return, i.e. those grossed up expenses serve as the basis/proxy for input VAT/GST recovery. This could be supported by the use of industry standard rates to determine the correct grossing up rebate rate. Such an approach has the potential to simplify VAT/GST compliance for eligible providers and further incentivise them to file income tax returns to access their VAT/GST input tax credits. Hence it could promote the providers' engagement with the tax system in general and improve the integrity of the tax system.

These schemes have the potential to simplify compliance for small sharing/gig economy operators while enhancing competitive neutrality by bringing them into the VAT/GST system and require them to charge the normal VAT/GST on their outputs. Neutrality may however not be achieved entirely under the flat-rate and lump-sum variations of a presumptive scheme, to the extent that non-eligible actors performing similar economic activities will have to charge the (most probably higher) VAT/GST rate that normally applies to this activity. Any such variations will however be the result of a trade-off between bringing sharing/gig economy providers within the VAT/GST net while mitigating any disproportionate compliance burden for micro-businesses and SMEs and promoting compliance. Neutrality could be enhanced by giving all businesses that perform economic equivalent activities (traditional as well as sharing/gig economy actors) and that meet the relevant criteria access to those schemes.

A jurisdiction may also consider coupling the operation of a presumptive scheme with a VAT/GST collection and/or liability role on other actors in the sharing/gig economy supply chain (e.g. digital platforms), as appropriate (see under 3.2.4, 3.3.6 and 3.3.7).

Further design and operation considerations

Turnover (e.g., the previous year) is the most common criterion for determining eligibility for a presumptive scheme. Its appeal will rely on the fact that almost every taxpayer concerned will have a broad idea of the expected value of its activities, therefore making it relatively easy to use and comply with. Even though other specific indicators per sector could also be taken into account for determining the eligibility for a presumptive scheme (e.g., the type of properties provided for short-term leasing, the number of journeys performed, etc.) it is recognised that these specific indicators could increase complexity and the associated administration and compliance burdens.

These schemes could be considered as an opt-in scheme. Some businesses may prefer to accurately claim the input VAT/GST that they have effectively incurred under normal rules, notably in cases where a high initial investment is necessary for a sharing/gig economy activity (e.g. drivers are required by the platform to use relatively new vehicles that meet specific standards) or where they operate predominantly for business customers. They may wish to opt for the application of the normal regime rather than for a presumptive scheme. Caution needs to be exercised to avoid abusive use of opt-in schemes by "fly-by-night" providers that may use those schemes on an *ad hoc* basis to gain undue advantages). For this reason, imposing a minimum period of time during which taxpayers that have opted for a scheme should remain under the scheme could be further considered as an anti-abuse measure.

While presumptive schemes have the potential to facilitate compliance for sharing/gig economy providers, care should be taken to ensure that these schemes are sufficiently simple to operate and monitor so that they do not create their own compliance risks and administrative burdens. Where presumptive schemes are complex, the need for a sharing/gig economy provider to monitor compliance with eligibility criteria, to understand the different applicable rules, and to regularly assess the benefit of a simplified scheme compared to the application of the normal regime in order to stay competitive with operators that operate under normal rules, could introduce complexity that may outweigh the benefit of simplification for eligible taxpayers. Business customers of sharing/gig economy providers that operate under a presumptive scheme may have difficulty determining the amounts of deductible VAT/GST included in the price paid to these providers, as it may vary along the VAT/GST rate that is applicable under the provider's presumptive scheme. Business customers may have difficulty adjusting their accounting systems to deal with this complexity and choose not to contract with providers that operate under a presumptive scheme. Finally, for sharing/gig economy platforms, it may be complex to manage the impact of various presumptive schemes that their underlying providers may operate under, e.g. on pricing, on the calculation of fees and commissions, etc. It is therefore important to regularly monitor the efficiency and effectiveness of presumptive VAT/GST schemes and to consult with the sectors involved to ensure a good understanding of emerging trends, opportunities and challenges with respect to their operation.

3.2.3. Registration, accounting and reporting simplification measures

This section outlines a number of additional options for tax authorities to consider in simplifying VAT/GST compliance and administration to accommodate the entry into the VAT/GST system of the new and often small businesses operating in the sharing/gig economy. These measures are essentially aimed at making the tax compliance process more straightforward and seamless for taxpayers. Simplification of compliance obligations can be an effective way of driving compliance, particularly for small businesses that may have less capacity to comply.

VAT/GST registration

Jurisdictions are encouraged to use technology to facilitate registration. This could include the possibility for taxpayers to manage their registration online through a single web-portal; limiting requirements for hard-copy documents; and the availability of online taxpayer support. Within a whole-of-government approach, the VAT/GST registration could be integrated with the registration processes for other governmental agencies/entities (a "one-stop-shop" approach with one single registration for multiple purposes).

Accounting and reporting simplification measures.

Accounting and reporting simplification measures that jurisdictions may wish to consider include:

- *limiting the reporting and record-keeping obligation for taxpayers to what is strictly required to calculate the final VAT/GST liability;*
- *limiting taxpayers' obligation to issue normal invoices* except where the customer specifically asks for one;
- *reduce the frequency of filing requirements.* The requirement to file and remit the VAT/GST at less frequent intervals is likely to reduce compliance costs and support eligible taxpayers' cash-flow. It is recognised though that less frequent filing and payment (e.g., annually) may increase the risk of the taxpayer being unable to pay a large amount of VAT/GST due and therefore such approach could benefit from a regular analysis of taxpayers' risk profile;
- *allow the optional use of cash accounting schemes,* i.e., schemes that allow taxpayers to defer their VAT/GST payments until they have collected payment from their customers. These schemes can support taxpayers' cash flow, while simplifying their VAT/GST accounting and providing automatic bad-debt relief. These regimes are often accompanied by a restriction on input tax deduction until payment of the input VAT/GST due has been made which may make them a less attractive option in certain cases. It is recognised that these schemes may be less

relevant for sharing/gig economy providers where the payment will often be made at the time of the supply (or even before) or shortly after;

- *facilitate the use of accounting and tax reporting software solutions by taxpayers.* The introduction of electronically enabled reporting and/or invoicing processes can bring benefits of greater accuracy and efficiency compared to paper-based processes, particularly where those solutions can be used to facilitate and simplify tax compliance. The presumed familiarity of sharing/gig economy actors with technology, and on their possible access to technology via the sharing/gig economy platforms that facilitate their activities, may create significant opportunities for the use of accounting and reporting software solutions to facilitate VAT/GST compliance. This could include the use of accounting software allowing micro and small businesses to record business-to-consumer transactions (B2C), possibly online and in real time, and generate pre-filled tax returns. These solutions could also include virtual low-cost cash registers that require basic IT infrastructure, e.g. only a mobile phone (often used by the sharing/gig economy providers). The report of the OECD Forum of Tax Administration on *Implementing Online Cash Registers: Benefits, Considerations and Guidance* is of great relevance in this context and provides further useful insights for interested jurisdictions to consider (OECD, 2019[2]).

The development of those software solutions will generally benefit from close co-operation with software developers and providers to determine the required set of information and provide the requirements of the tax rules that should be built into the software solutions to be used by taxpayers.

Such accounting software may allow the pre-population of (simplified) VAT/GST returns and transaction listings for submission to the tax authorities, thereby achieving productivity gains and improving the accuracy of their submissions. Considering the potential benefits of those software solutions while mitigating the associated compliance costs for taxpayers with limited capacity to comply, jurisdictions may consider making such software solutions available for free to taxpayers to assist and further incentivise their use.

3.2.4. Split payment/withholding VAT/GST collection mechanisms

The terms "split payment" and "withholding" are used interchangeably in this section to refer to a collection mechanism whereby the VAT/GST due on a sharing/gig economy transaction is collected/withheld via another party than the sharing/gig provider in the supply chain on behalf of the underlying sharing/gig provider.

This section considers the application of a split payment/withholding collection mechanism involving (i) financial intermediaries and (ii) the business customer in a sharing/gig economy supply chain.

Split payment/withholding of VAT/GST by financial intermediaries

Under a collection mechanism through split payment/withholding by financial intermediaries[3] in the sharing/gig economy supply chain, the latter are required to split/withhold the amount of the VAT/GST from the total price paid for a sharing/gig economy supply by the customer to the provider at the time of processing the payment.

Such a regime may appear as an attractive option for a number of reasons. It can simplify VAT/GST accounting for taxpayers particularly in case where transactions are carried out via digital means (e.g. online ordering and payment for transportation service). It minimises risks of VAT/GST revenue losses from non-compliance, fraud or insolvency for tax authorities as taxpayers do not handle the VAT/GST. However, a range of challenges and systemic weaknesses have been identified that can heavily limit the effectiveness or even the operational feasibility of such a regime. These challenges include:

- Financial intermediaries may often not have all the information necessary to fulfil the split payment or withholding obligation correctly. This includes information on the applicable

VAT/GST rate in jurisdictions that apply multiple rates; possible exemptions; details of prices calculation, whether a payment is subject to the split payment/withholding requirement (e.g., because the recipient of the payment is not the person liable for the VAT/GST). A financial intermediary will also generally not be able to process the VAT/GST aspects of a full or partial refund. To address these challenges, the sharing/gig economy provider, or the person that has VAT/GST liability, would need to use a dedicated bank account for its sharing/gig economy activities under the assumption that all payments to that account are subject to split payment/withholding at a given VAT/GST rate. Sharing/gig economy platforms may then make providers' access to their platform conditional upon the use of such a dedicated bank account to ensure these providers' compliance with their VAT/GST obligations.

- As often multiple financial intermediaries are involved in sharing/gig economy supply chains (credit card company, payment service provider, customer's bank, provider's bank, etc.) it will often be challenging for each of these intermediaries to know whether or not it has a split payment/withholding obligation. Clear rules will be required in this respect, which will inevitably add another layer of complexity.
- Tax authorities need access to information to monitor compliance with the split payment or withholding obligation, and to ensure the proper VAT/GST treatment of transactions that are not covered by the split payment/withholding regime (e.g. because alternative payment mechanisms were used) and of VAT/GST refunds for cancelled or refunded transactions. Tax authorities may need to turn to the sharing/gig economy platform or to other parties to gain proper insight in the full compliance picture.
- Taxpayers may face difficulties in adjusting their VAT/GST reporting and the calculation of VAT/GST liability in respect of the supplies for which VAT/GST has already been paid to the tax authorities through the split payment/withholding regime. Taxpayers may be relieved from the requirement to report transactions subject to the split payment/withholding regime, but that may limit the tax authorities' access to information that may be required for proper monitoring and audit (see previous bullet). Tax administrations will need to work closely with accountancy software developers to ensure the proper processing of the VAT/GST relevant aspects of transactions subject to a split payment/withholding regime.
- A split payment/withholding mechanism reduces the amount of the taxpayer's output VAT/GST, which is problematic for taxpayers that regularly incur deductible input VAT/GST. As there will be less output VAT/GST against which deductible input VAT/GST can be offset, such a taxpayer can find itself in a structural excess input tax credit position. This can crate cash-flow pressures which can be particularly challenging for small sharing/gig economy operators. These adverse consequences could be mitigated by limiting the split payment/withholding obligation to only part of the VA/GST amount, so that a share of the output VAT/GST can still be used by the provider to offset deductible input VAT/GST, at the cost of introducing an even greater level of complexity into the system.
- Compliance costs, and associated risks, for financial intermediaries may be considerable which may be passed on to sharing/gig economy operators and customers.
- A split payment/withholding regime is likely to incentivise the use of alternative payment options that are outside the traditional and/or national banking system (where available) and that may not be captured by a collection obligation that is typically imposed on domestic banks and other intermediaries in the jurisdiction of taxation. It may also incentivise the use of cash payments which remain the main payment modality in several jurisdictions (notably in developing economies)
- This regime may have an impact for customers, which may notably face difficulty to receive a full refund in case of errors or a cancelled transaction.

While it is clear that the operation of such a split payment/withholding as a primary collection mechanism faces significant challenges, a jurisdiction may wish to consider a collection role for financial intermediaries as a fall back option to enhance enforcement in cases where the person that has primary VAT/GST liability does not comply with its VAT/GST obligations (see Chapter 4).

Split payment/withholding of VAT/GST by business customers

The users of sharing/gig economy services may be predominantly private individuals, as explained in Chapter 1. Business customer however use sharing/gig economy services too, and this may increase over time as the sharing/gig economy continues to develop and differentiate. Against this background, the paragraphs below discuss the possible application of a split payment/withholding regime for collecting the VAT/GST on the supplies of sharing/gig economy services to the users, when those are business customers.

Under such a mechanism, the business customer of a sharing/gig economy supply acts as a splitting/withholding agent by separating the amount of the VAT/GST due for the supply from the net price at the time of payment and remitting this VAT/GST amount to the tax authority or on a dedicated account. If the customer is a fully taxable business, it is then entitled to deduct the VAT/GST that it has split and remitted to the tax authorities in accordance with normal VAT/GST rules. Such a system is similar to a self-assessment/reverse charge mechanism, with a number of differences. The cash-flow impact of a split-payment/withholding regime differs in that the business customer effectively remits the VAT/GST due on the sharing/gig economy supply to the tax authorities and recovers it separately via its VAT/GST return (as opposed to a self-assessment/reverse charge regime where the VAT/GST is normally reported as payable and deductible in the same return). Also the VAT/GST liability may be different in that it normally remains at the level of the supplier/provider in a split payment/withholding regime whereas it lies with the business customer under a self-assessment/reverse-charge mechanism.

Such a regime can be particularly helpful in facilitating compliance for sharing/gig economy providers transacting mainly with business customers. Examples could include food deliverers transacting directly with restaurants and/or a digital platform for the delivery of food; owners of real estate (apartments, houses) renting out their apartment/house directly to a hotel chain that subsequently offers stays there to final consumers. Under a split payment/withholding regime, the restaurant and the hotel in these examples would be required to split/withhold the VAT/GST due on the supply acquired from the sharing/gig economy provider (the food deliverer and the owner of the real estate) and remit it to the tax authorities. The role of a splitting/withholding agent could also be assumed by digital platforms that act as a principal in a sharing/gig economy supply, i.e. that receive the supply from the sharing/gig economy provider and supply it onwards to the final customer in their own name.

This approach relieves the sharing/gig economy provider from the burden of having to collect and remit the VAT/GST on its supplies by moving the VAT/GST payment liability to the business customer. This could generally be considered as a feasible and appropriate option as it can be assumed that business customers will have the information on the transaction that is necessary for a correct taxing decision and they have control over the payment.

Such a split payment/withholding approach may be attractive for a number of reasons. Once sharing/gig economy providers have been able to ascertain that they are subject to VAT/GST, it has the potential to simplify VAT/GST compliance for the providers that may have limited capacity to do so and thus increase overall compliance levels for tax authorities. It also facilitates the VAT/GST deduction for business customers as they have access to the necessary evidence for the payment of the VAT/GST while it reduces risks of fraud from the deduction of unpaid VAT/GST. For tax authorities, the costs of VAT/GST administration and compliance risks are reduced as VAT/GST is collected from a relatively small number of businesses that generally have the capacity to comply (e.g. restaurants; hotels;

platforms) instead of having to administer collection from large numbers of often small sharing/gig economy providers.

When considering the implementation of a split payment/withholding regime, tax authorities may wish to further consider the following aspects:

- While business customers can generally be presumed to have access to all the necessary information to carry out their split payment/withholding obligation and to have the capacity to comply, this may not always be the case notably for small businesses. Tax authorities may therefore consider excluding small businesses from a split payment/withholding obligation;
- Clear rules will be necessary to allow business customers to easily identify the transactions for which they have a split payment/withholding obligation and to distinguish these transactions from transactions that are out of scope. This may notably require a clear identification of sectors or categories of transactions that are within the scope of the split payment/withholding regime.
- Tax authorities may consider implementing a requirement for business customers to remit the VAT/GST due under a split payment/withholding regime periodically rather than on a transaction-by-transaction basis.
- A split payment/withholding mechanism reduces the amount of output VAT/GST for providers that are subject to such a regime and thus reduces the amount of VAT/GST against which deductible input VAT/GST can be credited. This can lead to cash-flow pressures for particularly small businesses that regularly incur deductible input VAT/GST. Tax authorities may consider ways to ensure a simple and rapid process for refunding such amounts of excess input VAT/GST.
- Compliance with a split payment/withholding regime could be further simplified by combining it with simplified accounting and reporting obligations for the sharing/gig economy providers (see 3.2.3 above) and/or a presumptive tax scheme (which removes the need for sharing/gig economy providers to claim input VAT/GST deduction for individual expense items).

3.2.5. Technology-based data collection to facilitate VAT/GST administration

Technology is an integral part of the sharing/gig economy. Section 3.2.3. considered the role of technology in promoting and facilitating compliance notably via the use of tax software solutions and digitally enabled registration and reporting processes. This section focuses in particular on the use of technology for data collection by tax authorities to enhance compliance risk management and facilitate compliance for sharing/gig economy actors.

Information technologies are available to facilitate the collection of data to support VAT/GST administration and risk management in the sharing/gig economy. A wide set of IT techniques are available for VAT/GST administrations, such as web scraping or web crawling tools, to monitor the sharing/gig economy. These tools can be used by tax administrations to search the Internet for sites that offer or promote sharing/gig economy activities or to extract ("scrape") VAT/GST relevant information from certain public sources (including sites operated by sharing/gig economy platforms). These tools can be (further) developed or tailored in-house tools to take into account the specific features of data to be collected from particular platforms or third parties. Such data collected from the Internet can include information on individual transactions including the identity of a sharing/gig economy provider, or contact details such as a telephone number or an email address that allows the tax administration to identify providers (e.g. though automatic cross-checking of telephone number with telephone directories).

This data can be used for a range of tax administration actions, including:

- monitoring the development of the sharing/gig economy, including the emergence of new sector, the evolution of existing sectors and their business models, and the associated compliance and revenue risks;
- strengthen VAT/GST risk analysis capacity in respect of the sharing/gig economy through the use of data analytics notably to identify taxpayers and/or taxpayer segments that may need a targeted approach;
- to analyse the impact of changes in tax policy on compliance and taxpayer behaviour, e.g. changes in registration or collection thresholds or in the frequency of return filing and VAT/GST payment;
- rolling out information campaigns to enhance voluntary compliance by sharing/gig economy operators, including through direct communication with sharing/gig economy providers (e.g. via letters, e-mails or social media). For the use of technology to support education and dissemination of information to promote compliance, see 3.2.7 below.

A number of challenges and limitations associated with the collection of these data, their quality and use by tax authorities need to be highlighted, in particular:

- tax authorities may not have access to the VAT/GST relevant information until after a transaction has taken place, e.g., the address of an immovable property that is offered for short-time rental may become available only after a booking has been made via a booking platform;
- Tax authorities may not be able to use the data collected from the Internet immediately, but will first need to check its reliability and transform into a dataset with the appropriate structure to support data analysis (including the capacity to identify unique taxpayers), and finally to ensure secure storage of these data as appropriate. These processes, include training and recruitment of skilful personnel, can be resource-intensive;
- web scraping tools for the extraction of information from Internet sites and platforms, may need to be adjusted for each site or platform. Challenges may include the use of techniques by platforms or sites (e.g. "captcha" mechanisms) to prevent the automatic extraction of information by their competitors; and techniques to protect the identity of the providers behind the offers on their platform.

To address these challenges and limitations, tax authorities are encouraged to consult with sharing/gig economy platforms and other stakeholders that may hold useful information (e.g. financial intermediaries) to enhance the potential and efficiency of technology based data collection. This could also include consultation with developers and providers of accounting and tax software solutions (which could be certified by the tax authorities) to ensure that the VAT/GST relevant data are structured in a way that allows for direct transmission to the tax authorities without the need for further manipulation or that they can be collected directly by the tax administration from the taxpayers' systems, e.g. through an "application-programming interface" (API).

Overall new IT technologies could enable moving away from traditional reporting and assessment processes towards more compliance-by-design outcomes,[4] which have great potential in facilitating compliance and administration while drastically reducing opportunities for non-compliance.

3.2.6. Reporting obligations for third parties

Section 3.2.5. discusses the possible use of technology by tax authorities to collect VAT/GST relevant data from the internet to enhance compliance risk management in the sharing/gig economy and facilitate compliance for sharing/gig economy actors. Chapter 4 further discusses the role of data in supporting enforcement and compliance monitoring.

This section looks in further detail at the possibility for tax authorities to collect information through a reporting obligation for other stakeholders in the sharing/gig economy supply chain than the persons that are liable to collect and remit the VAT/GST on a sharing/gig economy supply.

Such third parties in sharing/gig economy activities could involve the financial intermediaries, sharing/gig economy platforms, or parties acting on behalf of a sharing/gig economy provider (e.g. real estate agents that administer immovable property on behalf of multiple owners and who may contract directly with sharing/gig economy platforms). Section 3.3. of this Chapter presents a detailed analysis of the role of sharing/gig economy platforms in tax authorities' data collection strategies. This includes a detailed discussion on the VAT/GST dimension of the *Model Rules for Reporting by Platform Operators with respect to Sellers in the Sharing and Gig Economy*, which were released by the OECD in 2020 (OECD, 2020[3]).

When considering reporting obligations for these third parties, it is important that tax authorities take stock of the VAT/GST relevant information that is already available via other sources, particularly the information reported by the primary actors in the sharing/gig economy supply chain (providers and sharing/gig platforms) who may presumably be best placed to provide sufficient and accurate relevant information (see available information elements in Annex D). This will be helpful in minimising risks of duplication and complexity in reporting obligations.

The following overarching VAT/GST design policy principles may further be useful for tax authorities to consider when designing a possible reporting requirement for third parties in the sharing/gig economy:

- *Have a clear understanding of the policy objective pursued* when determining the type and amount of the data to be reported. This is of crucial importance to ensure an efficient and proportionate operation of reporting obligations, recognising that new data reporting requirements come at a cost both for the administration and for the third parties that will have to report;
- *Identify the right data sources.* An appropriate identification of the data sources is important both to ensure the relevance and adequacy of the data collected as well as to minimize the associated administrative and compliance burden. To this end administrations could explore opportunities to facilitate cooperation and information exchange amongst domestic public agencies so as to minimise the risks of unnecessary duplication of reporting requirements;
- *Consult with stakeholders* concerned/involved (including IT/software providers) from the outset of the process so as to ensure a good understanding of their business processes and information available and to set up the appropriate environment (including specific reporting formats) in a workable and proportionate manner;
- *Ensure adequate human and technical resources* to securely handle/process the (big) volumes of collected information and produce effective analysis in a timely fashion;
- *Develop a robust legal framework* so as to ensure the appropriate compatibility of reporting rules with other regulatory areas (e.g. data protection/privacy/competition related) and to support their effective operation and enforcement;
- *Leverage on technology-enabled solutions* to ensure the reliability of the transmitted data and their reporting in a timely manner while mitigating administration and compliance costs. This includes the possible use of Application Programming Interfaces (APIs) that allow the administration's systems to digitally interact with the systems of third parties subject to reporting obligations;
- *Maximize consistency across jurisdictions* with respect to the information elements collected as well as reporting formats. This will facilitate and enhance compliance, particularly for third parties that are faced with multi-jurisdictional reporting obligations, reduce compliance costs

and improve the effectiveness and quality of information sharing mechanisms. For tax authorities consistency is also likely to support the effective international co-operation and enforcement.

3.2.7. Promoting compliance through communication, information and education

As discussed under Chapter 1 of this report, individual sharing/gig economy providers may often not be fully aware of their tax obligations and/or have limited capacity to comply as they may have little access to easy-to-understand information and to assistance by tax professionals. Actions by tax authorities to raise awareness among sharing/gig economy actors and to educate them on VAT/GST and other tax obligations are therefore of great importance to promote voluntary compliance.

It is recognised at the outset that educational tools work best if the rules are simple for the suppliers to comply with. Therefore, a jurisdiction may need to focus first on the implementation of simplification measures and then support their operation through education and communication.

Communication is critical for tax systems to promote compliance. Tax administration's strategies in this context typically include publishing relevant information concerning tax regimes and obligations and compliance guidance on a dedicated tax authority website and targeted information campaigns including through social media. Tax authorities may consider creating dedicated web pages or portals for sharing/gig economy operators setting out the VAT/GST obligations and possible simplification regimes that may be available. Sharing/gig economy platforms could post links to this information on their website.

Theoretical information education may not always be sufficient, particularly in communication with sharing/gig economy providers. Additional and targeted communication and support efforts have been found to be effective in raising awareness and supporting compliance including the release of videos explaining VAT/GST registration and compliance processes; dedicated training sessions possibly organised in co-operation with sharing/gig economy platforms; and a dedicated "hotline" to answer to specific questions.

The information provided by tax authorities should obviously be reliable, timely, and easy to access and to understand. Experience suggests that the impact and usefulness of VAT/GST information can be enhanced considerably by making it available in a jurisdictions' main trading languages in addition to the national language. This may for instance facilitate the education of sharing/gig economy providers on the VAT/GST obligations by sharing/gig economy platforms, which may often be established abroad, and allow these to assist sharing/gig economy providers in complying with heir VAT/GST obligations for the activities that they carry out through their platform.

Digital platforms facilitating sharing/gig economy activities have an important role to play in this context which is further discussed under Section 3.3.

3.3. The potential roles for digital platforms to address the VAT/GST implications of the sharing/gig economy

This section of the report focuses on the potential roles for digital platforms in enhancing compliance by sharing/gig economy providers with the VAT/GST obligations in respect of their sharing/gig economy supplies. This section thus considers situations where a sharing/gig economy platform operator is not liable itself for the VAT/GST obligations in respect of the sharing/gig economy activities carried out through its platform under normal VAT/GST rules. This section does notably not apply to platforms that are regarded as the provider of a sharing/gig economy supply under a jurisdiction's VAT/GST rules. This section does apply to sharing/gig economy platforms that are considered to act as agents, including for VAT/GST purposes, by enabling a direct interaction between sharing/gig economy providers and users with respect to a sharing/gig economy supply that is considered to take place between these two parties. In return, such a sharing/gig economy platform may receive a consideration/fee from either the provider or the user or both.

The 2019 Digital Platforms report considered a number of potential roles for digital platforms in the collection of VAT/GST on online sales (OECD, 2019[1]). This report focused in particular on e-commerce sales of services and digital products (such as streaming of music and movies, software application, etc.) and on online retail sales of goods (including the importation of small parcels from online sales). This report also took note of the prominent role of digital platforms in the growth of the sharing/gig economy and the desire of tax authorities to consider the potential role of platforms in enhancing VAT/GST compliance in this context (see Section 1.3.3. of the 2019 Digital Platforms Report (OECD, 2019[1])). The report recognised, however, that the sharing/gig economy was a relatively new and rapidly evolving phenomenon with specific features, and that further research and analysis were required on the possible impact of its growth on VAT/GST policy and administration before any conclusions could be drawn about the possible role of digital platforms in addressing these VAT/GST aspects. The 2019 Digital Platforms report therefore concluded that additional work on the sharing/gig economy would be carried out as a separate work stream, in consultation with the sharing/gig economy stakeholders and taking account of the findings and recommendations included in the 2019 report (OECD, 2019[1]).

The table below recalls and outlines the main similarities and specificities of the sharing/gig economy compared to the broader digital platform economy that may warrant specific consideration when evaluating the roles that digital platforms may play in addressing the VAT/GST implications of the sharing/gig economy growth.

Table 3.1. Sharing/gig economy vs. broader platform economy

Similarities	Specificities of the sharing/gig economy
• Digital platforms play a critical role in facilitating the supplies via the use of advanced technology. • The underlying supplies are not new but the means through which they are carried out are. • The platforms have a relation with both the underlying provider and the consumer. They are "multi-sided" platforms in that they enable the direct interaction between two or more customers or participant groups (typically users/customers and providers) whereby each group of participants ("side") are customers of the multi-sided platform in some meaningful way. • Digital platforms have access to VAT/GST relevant information in the course of their normal business activity. • Digital platforms generally do not have a physical presence in the jurisdiction of taxation. • An increasing number of jurisdictions have already enacted legislation involving digital platforms in the collection of VAT/GST on online sales or are in the process of doing so.	• The sharing/gig economy typically involves transactions carried out by large numbers of new economic operators, which did not carry out activities within the scope of VAT/GST before starting their sharing/gig economy activity, and which may have limited knowledge of the VAT/GST legislation and limited capacity to comply with VAT/GST obligations. • Sharing/gig economy suppliers may be individuals or small businesses that generate relatively small turnover from their sharing/gig economy activities. • Sharing/gig economy activity may often involve high volumes of low-value transactions (for instance in the transportation sector). • The underlying sharing/gig economy providers have often a (type of) presence in the jurisdiction of taxation and are less likely to provide their services in multiple jurisdictions. • The sharing/gig economy supplies often involve physical assets/capital of a certain value in the jurisdiction of taxation (e.g. a vehicle or an immovable property in the currently dominant sectors of transportation and accommodation). • The underlying sharing/gig economy providers often use assets for both their sharing/gig economy activities and for private purposes. • A wide(r) range of VAT/GST policy objectives may be pursued by the tax authorities in respect of the

Similarities	Specificities of the sharing/gig economy
	sharing/gig economy than purely levying VAT/GST on these activities (e.g. monitoring market evolutions).

The various roles for digital platforms in supporting VAT/GST collection as identified in the 2019 Digital Platforms report are considered further in this section in light of the specifics of the sharing/gig economy outlined above (OECD, 2019[1]). The following roles for digital platforms in facilitating and enhancing VAT/GST compliance in the sharing/gig economy will be considered in particular:

- educating sharing/gig economy providers on their VAT/GST obligations;
- data reporting to the tax authorities to facilitate compliance (e.g. by pre-filling VAT/GST returns) and/or preventing non-compliance by sharing/gig economy providers;
- assuming a type of liability for the collection of VAT/GST on the sharing/gig economy supplies they facilitate.

Table 3.2. below provides a more detailed overview of these roles with a focus on their key features and the possible policy objective(s) that each role may address. Each of these roles comes with its own challenges and opportunities, which are considered in further detail in the remaining part of this section together with an outline of broader design considerations.

While the order by which those roles are presented and discussed in this section does not suggest a particular preference or priority, it does reflect a number of considerations including:

- the possibility that jurisdictions may wish to adopt a gradual VAT/GST policy approach, or a differentiated sectoral approach, which is likely to influence the possible role of sharing/gig economy platforms in supporting that policy;
- the possibility that a jurisdiction may not necessarily want to levy VAT/GST on all sharing/gig economy activities and may for instance first wish to monitor this economy's development and the possible need for further VAT/GST policy action;
- the potential preference for a jurisdiction to limit compliance burdens for digital platforms and/or to implement role(s) that have the potential for application to a broader number of platforms and/or are more future proof in view of emerging business models;
- a jurisdiction's capacity to administer VAT/GST compliance and collection in the sharing/gig economy in the absence of the involvement of sharing/gig economy platforms in the VAT/GST process.

Table 3.2. Overview of potential roles for digital platforms in addressing the VAT/GST implications of the sharing/gig economy

Role	Broad description	Key features and variations (not always mutually exclusive)	Policy objective to be addressed (design dependent)
Educational and Communication Role	Digital platforms serve as communication channels to provide accurate and timely information to sharing/gig economy providers on their VAT/GST obligations.	It can be performed either spontaneously by the digital platforms or in close co-operation with the tax authorities. It is intended to supplement rather than replace existing communication strategies by tax authorities to inform (potential) taxpayers of their obligations.	• Help promote and facilitate appropriate levels of compliance by sharing/gig economy providers. • Level the playing field for compliant actors.
Formal Co-operation Agreements	Formal co-operation agreements can be multi-faceted in that they can combine a variety of measures and approaches to involve digital platforms in VAT/GST compliance by underlying sharing/gig economy providers.	Formal co-operation agreements typically include: • information sharing (on demand or regular); and • education (including the platform serving as a conduit to communicate with underlying sharing/gig economy providers on their VAT/GST compliance obligations); • alerting the tax authorities and platforms for instance of suspected non-compliance and/or fraud; • responding quickly to notifications by a tax authority of underlying sharing/gig economy suppliers that are found to be in breach of their VAT/GST obligations.	• Promote/facilitate compliance by sharing/gig economy suppliers. • Level the playing field for compliant actors. • Enhance tax authorities' effectiveness and efficiency.
Information Sharing Role	The digital platform is required by law to provide the tax authority with information relevant for VAT/GST purposes without the platform necessarily being liable or having a role in collecting and remitting the VAT/GST due on the sharing/gig economy supply.	• Provision of information on request: the digital platform is required to retain records of VAT/GST relevant information so that this information can be made available to the tax authority on request; e.g. per provider and category of supplies, in cases of suspicious activity…; • Systematic provision of information: the digital platform is systematically and periodically required to provide information on supplies carried out via the platform, to or accessible by the jurisdiction of taxation.	• Monitor the size and impact of the sharing/gig economy. • Estimate any potential risk of VAT/GST base erosion. • Enhance the efficiency of VAT/GST administration including assist the tax authority in detecting/deterring non-compliance and those involved; • Facilitate/promote compliance by the liable sharing/gig economy provider(s); • Level the playing field for compliant

Role	Broad description	Key features and variations (not always mutually exclusive)	Policy objective to be addressed (design dependent)
			actors.
Joint and Several Liability (JSL)	If the underlying sharing/gig economy provider is not VAT/GST compliant, the JSL regime provides the possibility for the tax authorities to declare the platform that facilitates the sharing/gig economy supply jointly and severally liable for the VAT/GST due.	• Variation 1: the platform is held jointly and severally liable for the future undeclared VAT/GST by the underlying suppliers, once the tax authority has spotted cases of non-compliance, has reported these cases to the digital platform and the latter did not take appropriate action within a specified number of days. Such action by the digital platform typically consists of securing compliance from the underlying provider or removing the provider from its platform. • Variation 2: the sharing/gig economy platform may be held jointly and severally liable for the past undeclared VAT/GST for the underlying provider when the digital platform should have had a reasonable expectation based on the underlying provider's activities on the platform that the provider should be registered for VAT/GST but has not. It is for the taxing jurisdiction to determine when such a reasonable expectation exists.	• Promote/facilitate compliance by sharing/gig economy providers. • Level the playing field with compliant actors.
Collection/Withholding Role	The sharing/gig economy platform acts on behalf of the underlying sharing/gig economy provider to calculate, collect and remit the VAT/GST due on the supplies carried out through its platform.	The platform incurs no wider liability towards the tax authorities than to pass on the VAT/GST collected on the supplies carried out by the underlying sharing/gig economy providers. These underlying suppliers remain liable for the VAT/GST towards the tax authorities. Depending on the design, the underlying provider may still need to fulfil his/her VAT/GST reporting obligations (i.e. the only relief is the payment of the VAT/GST that has already been collected and remitted to the tax authority by the platform).	• Promote/facilitate compliance by sharing/gig economy providers. • Level the playing field with compliant actors.

Role	Broad description	Key features and variations (not always mutually exclusive)	Policy objective to be addressed (design dependent)
Full Liability Role (FLR)	The digital platform is designated by the law as the VAT/GST liable supplier. Under this role the digital platform is solely and fully liable for assessing, collecting and remitting the VAT/GST on the sharing/gig economy activity that goes through the platform, to the tax authorities in the jurisdiction of taxation, in line with the VAT/GST legislation of that jurisdiction. This liability is limited to VAT/GST obligations only. It does not affect any other liability aspects for the sharing/gig economy platform beyond the VAT/GST.	The digital platform assumes full VAT/GST liability as if it has itself carried out the supply by the underlying sharing/gig provider. The underlying sharing/gig economy provider is in principle relieved from any VAT/GST liability in respect of its supply to the sharing/gig economy customer/user. • Variation 1: The FLR applies only in cases where the underlying provider is regarded as a taxable person for VAT/GST purposes under the national law. • Variation 2: The FLR applies irrespective of the status of the underlying supplier for VAT/GST purposes under the national law. This variation 2 could notably apply in cases were the platform is considered as having a de facto employment relationship with the underlying supplier under the applicable labor laws. In order to avoid a break in the staged collection chain, the full VAT/GST liability regime may treat the digital platform as having received the supply from the underlying sharing/gig economy provider and having supplied it onwards to the final customer/user.	• Broaden/protect the tax base; • Level the playing field for compliant operators • Enhance the efficiency of the VAT/GST administration. • Facilitate/enhance compliance.

Source: OECD analysis

3.3.1. Scope and operation of digital platforms' involvement in addressing the VAT/GST implications of the sharing/gig economy

Which platform to be enlisted under which role? Determining eligibility

This part of the analysis considers potential roles for the platforms that enable groups of sharing/gig economy providers and users to interact directly and to enter into transactions, through the use of the advanced technology that these platforms provide. It focuses on the digital platforms that carry out functions in the sharing/gig economy that can play an essential role in facilitating and enhancing VAT/GST compliance in respect of sharing/gig economy supplies.

In keeping with this approach, the analysis focuses on the possible approaches that a tax authority could use when determining the digital platforms it wishes to involve in the VAT/GST compliance process under a potential role. The starting point for this is to consider what is required for a digital platform to be able to comply with a specific role depending on the policy objective set. Overall whether a digital platform is indeed in a position to comply with a specific role may often depend on its business model, and a targeted analysis and consultation with individual platforms would be therefore required.

Tax authorities are encouraged to issue clear guidance on the scope of the VAT/GST regime(s) for digital platforms in the sharing/gig economy in their jurisdiction. This could be provided by reference to the functions performed by digital platforms that take account of these platforms' capability to comply with a given role (see Annex E).

It is for tax authorities to decide on the level of detail they want to go into when providing guidance/indicators of digital platforms' inclusion in the scope of a role. Possible approaches include the use of list(s) of functions that are considered indicative of a digital platform's capability to take on a specific role (i.e. a positive list); and/or of digital platform's inability to take on a specific role (i.e. a negative list). The use of detailed indicators for platforms' inclusion in, or exclusion from, a specific role has the advantage of enhancing certainty for digital platforms and tax authorities. It may be challenging, however, for tax authorities to keep such detailed indicators up-to-date in light of the rapid evolution of sharing/gig economy business models and of information technology and the capability it provides to digital platforms to comply with VAT/GST obligations under a specific role/regime. This could result in an uneven playing field, where some digital platforms remain out of scope of a role on the basis of the indicators defined by a tax authority, although they are in fact in a similar position as platforms that are covered by the same role and have the capacity to comply with it, e.g. through the implementation of new technologies that are not yet reflected in these indicators. Same considerations are relevant in case that a jurisdiction decides to publish a list with names of digital platforms covered by a specific role. Such individual approach may lead to distortions in competition/arbitrary decisions based on tax authorities understanding of the market.

Against this background, tax authorities may wish to build in some flexibility when designing and implementing the indicators for the inclusion of digital platforms under a specific role. Apart from neutrality considerations, which require that digital platforms that are in a similar situation are treated equally, a flexible approach also allows tax authorities to give due consideration to the proportionality aspect. A platform may for instance be eligible for the application of a role on the basis of the functions it performs, whereas the application of this role would in fact result in disproportionate compliance burden given the platform's technological or financial capabilities. This may notably be the case for small and medium digital platforms and for start-ups. To avoid potential risks of uneven treatment of platforms that are in similar situation, such a flexible approach could be based on clear and robust criteria and any exclusion from a role be reviewed regularly so as to reflect any changes in the technological or financial capacities of the digital platform concerned. Special consideration will be required also in the context of a platform in platform ecosystem in terms of identifying which platform could be enlisted under a specific role (see further description under Annex D).

Additional consideration might also be given to how other rules than VAT/GST rules applicable to digital platforms may interact with conditions imposed under one of the potential roles considered in this report, e.g. reporting obligations on digital platforms that may already exist for direct tax purposes.

All the above considerations confirm the importance of tax authorities consulting closely with the digital platforms involved in the sharing/gig economy to achieve a good understanding of their ecosystems and trends so as to ensure the workability of platforms' roles in a proportionate and, to the extent possible, future proof manner.

Foreign platforms (i.e. operated by non-residents) vs. domestic platforms

In principle, it should not matter whether the sharing/gig economy platform is operated by a resident or by a non-resident of the jurisdiction of taxation. Consideration might be given however to the fact that enforcement might be more challenging against foreign digital platforms, and tax authorities might consider introducing additional (reasonable and proportionate) safeguards to reduce risks of non-compliance where appropriate (see further analysis below under Chapter 4).

Tax authorities may wish to give particularly careful consideration when considering a VAT/GST collection or liability role for platforms in respect of the sharing/gig economy activities they facilitate. As highlighted above, sharing/gig economy providers are often located in the jurisdiction of taxation and may already be registered there for VAT/GST purposes. This is different to the broader digital platforms economy, particularly e-commerce sales of goods, services and digital products, which may often involve online sellers that sell into markets around the world form a single location to. Where the sharing/gig economy platform is not located in the jurisdiction of taxation, the tax authorities may wish to carefully weigh the risks and benefits from shifting the VAT/GST collection or liability for sharing/gig supplies from the individual sharing/gig economy providers that are resident in its jurisdiction onto a platform that is not resident in this jurisdiction. This is further examined under the relevant sections for different roles of the platforms.

Voluntary or mandatory?

In theory most of the roles for platforms considered under this report (with the exception of the formal co-operation agreements roles) could be designed either as voluntary or mandatory. Each approach merits a number of considerations.

While optional and contractual roles have the benefit of flexibility, they may lead to the development of exceptional VAT/GST collection schemes that may vary from one platform to another and create uncertainty and complexity for compliance and administration. A proliferation of such a variety of schemes, and their optional character, may risk undermining efforts to secure VAT/GST compliance by actors that may seek to operate on platforms that have not entered into an optional regime or that operate an optional regime that involves less (perceived) VAT/GST compliance burdens than other regimes.

Optional sharing/gig economy roles may also create challenges for administrative co-operation and exchange of information between jurisdictions to the extent that there may be no definite legal status and obligation for the platform to comply with a role. Overall, a mandatory operation of a role on all eligible sharing/gig economy platforms will generally be more effective for tax administrations in enhancing VAT/GST compliance and in providing certainty and an even playing field for sharing/gig actors involved.

In the interim, a jurisdiction may consider running a (voluntary) pilot programme with sharing/gig economy platforms to test a possible regime, for instance as part of a cooperative agreement with platforms. This could ultimately facilitate the transition into a mandatory operation of such a role across all platforms concerned.

Other overarching design considerations

The involvement of digital platforms in the VAT/GST compliance process is not exempt from challenges from the point of view of risk assessment, tax monitoring, audits and compliance. In particular, as many of the (big) platforms may have no physical presence in the jurisdiction of consumption (taxing jurisdiction) that would allow an enforcement of domestic rules, there are inherent limitations to the effectiveness of those rules. Audit and risk management efforts face important limitations, as local legislation may be ineffective in enforcing them against non-resident platforms.

The ability to effectively enforce, i.e. ensure compliance by digital platforms under the VAT/GST roles imposed by the domestic legislation, is of crucial importance to avoid competitive distortion for compliant platforms that would result from compliance not being properly enforced against non-compliant foreign platforms. Poor enforcement could lead to underlying sharing/gig economy providers leaving compliant digital platforms for a digital platform that allows for non-compliant activity.

To address these challenges the tax authorities are encouraged to adopt a two-pronged approach whereby, on the one hand compliance is facilitated and encouraged by robust legal frameworks that build on the *Ottawa Taxation Framework Conditions* and on the other hand, appropriate deterrents are implemented against non-compliance.

In addition to the overarching design principles and considerations for a VAT/GST strategy targeted at the sharing/gig economy as outlined in Chapter 2, tax authorities are encouraged to take account of the following policy principles and considerations when designing potential role(s) for digital platforms in enhancing VAT/GST compliance in the sharing/gig economy:

- *Engage with the digital platforms early in the reform process*. Consultation with the digital platforms concerned allows tax authorities to achieve the appropriate understanding of the platforms' business models and operation, which will contribute to identifying solutions that are proportionate and workable. With respect to reporting obligations for instance, it is important to identify what type of information the digital platforms can reasonably be expected to provide to tax authorities to ensure that policy objectives can be met without disproportionate burden for digital platforms - recognising that available information may differ among platforms.
- *Provide appropriate lead-in time* in order to ensure that digital platforms will be in a position to comply with the role. It is likely that platforms will need to develop and implement considerable system changes to ensure appropriate levels of efficiency, certainty and effectiveness.
- *Promote compliance by limiting VAT/GST compliance obligations to what is strictly necessary* to facilitate the compliance process by digital platforms. Where compliance procedures are too complex and/or disproportionate, their application for digital platforms may lead to non-compliance or certain (non-resident) digital platforms declining to serve customers in certain jurisdictions. The compliance processes should therefore be as simple and efficient as possible. Where possible, simplified registration and compliance regimes such as those presented in the *International VAT/GST Guidelines* (OECD, 2017[4]) and the 2017 Report on *Mechanisms for the Collection of VAT/GST* (OECD, 2017[5]) are expected to facilitate compliance by digital platforms.
- *Wherever relevant, clearly define the VAT/GST obligations of the underlying sharing/gig economy providers*, notably in their relationship with the platform. This includes clear rules on the VAT/GST status of the relationship between the underlying provider and the digital platform;

the VAT/GST treatment of the platform fees; and the associated compliance obligations (invoicing, reporting, payment of VAT/GST, etc.). Similarly, consider providing clear guidance in cases where persons/entities are active on a platform under their own name but on behalf of other parties as undisclosed agents (e.g. a property manager that may act in its own name but on behalf of various homeowners as further illustrated in Annex D).

- *Provide clear guidance on the operation of any VAT/GST registration or collection thresholds.* Where a threshold exists in the jurisdiction of taxation it is important to be clear whether the threshold is set at the level of the platform or at the level of each underlying sharing/gig economy provider.
- *Consider implementing hierarchy rules in cases where more than one digital platform may be involved in the supply chain/ecosystem* (e.g. under a "platform on platform" scenario - this particular business model is further described in Annex D). Those rules should clarify which digital platform is enlisted under which specific role.
- *Depending on the situation, any reform might be best achieved through a phased implementation and/or grand-fathering provisions* for sharing/gig economy activities covered by a role before the law comes into effect for both the digital platforms and the national authorities involved.
- *Consider the need for rules to limit compliance risks for platforms acting in good faith and having made reasonable efforts to ensure compliance*, particularly in respect of the collection and verification of the information elements that platforms may have to report or base their tax determination on. Digital platforms must often rely on information provided to them by the underlying sharing/gig economy providers and third parties as appropriate to comply with their VAT/GST obligations under certain roles. There is therefore an expectation for platforms to operate meaningful due diligence processes in respect of the accuracy and the reliability of this information. In principle due diligence processes should ensure that accurate information is reported/used for VAT/GST related determinations without imposing overly burdensome procedures on platforms. The application of a rule that eliminates digital platforms' liability for mistakes resulting from reliance on inaccurate information can be considered reasonable, if the platform can provide evidence of its good faith and of its reasonable efforts to secure the accuracy and reliability of the information. This could include cases where the platform relies on a verification service by a jurisdiction's tax authorities to ascertain the identity and VAT/GST status of an underlying provider and/or user.
- *Consider moving from a transactions-based system for determining and validating the accuracy of VAT/GST related information to a systems-based validation system.* The use of business analytics may, over time, provide a more efficient solution for assessing VAT/GST compliance than the current practice of testing every individual transaction, including high-volume/low-value supplies. Moving to a systems-based approach will normally require that tax authorities acquire a good understanding of the relevant digital platforms, their business models and their business accounting and tax compliance systems.
- *Consider trade-related issues.* Tax authorities are expected to ensure that, in accordance with the *International VAT/GST Guidelines*, the domestic design and operation of roles involving foreign digital platforms do not unduly affect the international neutrality (OECD, 2017[4]). Guideline 2.6. according to which specific measures may be required for transactions involving foreign businesses also applies to digital platforms (OECD, 2017[4]). This Guideline clearly indicates, however, that such measures should not create disproportionate or inappropriate compliance burden (OECD, 2017[4]). Tax authorities are therefore encouraged to take due account of the approaches for a consistent design of regimes involving foreign platforms and for limiting compliance complexity as outlined in this analysis.

- *Consider a number of supporting measures for the efficient and effective operation of the roles for digital platforms* in facilitating VAT/GST compliance in the sharing/gig economy, including complementing these roles with robust international administrative co-operation; ensure deterrents for non-compliance; complement these roles with the targeted risk management strategies including through extensive use of third party data to assist compliance monitoring and data analysis; do not lose sight of similar activities that may be performed offline and/or with limited intervention of digital platforms (e.g. in cases where the platform operates as a click through/ referral platform thus enabling the discovery, promotion or listing of sharing/gig supplies by providers without any direct or indirect involvement of the digital platform in the setting of the terms of the underlying supply or in the payment or supply process). These supporting measures are discussed in further detail under Chapter 4 of this report.

3.3.2. Education/communication role

Under an education and communication role, sharing/gig economy platforms serve as communication channels to provide accurate and timely information to sharing/gig economy providers on their VAT/GST obligations. This could include the dissemination of guidelines and direct notifications on changes in obligations. Platforms can also develop their own guidance and documentation for their sharing/gig economy providers in consultation with the tax authorities.

Digital platforms can be encouraged to carry out such a role spontaneously or this could be organised in close co-operation with tax authorities, e.g. as part of a co-operation agreement. The enlistment of digital platforms under such an education/communication role will generally be intended to supplement rather than replace existing communication strategies by tax authorities to inform (potential) taxpayers of their obligations. The key policy objective being to promote and facilitate compliance and ultimately level the playing field for compliant actors.

Table 3.3. Education/Communication Role

Opportunities and challenges – Overview

Opportunities	Challenges
• Such a role provides **an opportunity for the tax authorities to communicate** with/reach out to the large number of underlying sharing/gig providers for the dissemination of information on VAT/GST obligations. • It increases the efficiency of communication on VAT/GST compliance with **taxpayers that may otherwise be often difficult to reach** by tax authorities. • **Cooperation with platforms allows for a proactive approach** in addressing questions from sharing/gig economy providers. • It helps those that want to comply and alerts those that are unaware. • It may induce providers **to comply and prevent them from making mistakes** that could lead to litigation and administrative burden for the tax authorities. • Enhance the **effective operation of other roles for digital platforms** (e.g. JSL, information sharing) and/or other broader policy options.	• **Tax authorities may lack the resources and/or technological capacity** to provide information in a timely manner and to keep that updated and accessible for platforms to disseminate. • For digital platforms, it could be **a challenge to ensure that they make the correct and up-to-date information available**, particularly across multiple sectors of the sharing/gig economy and while working with providers established in several jurisdictions (contact with the tax authorities in the platform's jurisdiction is likely to be insufficient in that respect). • Platforms would **need assurance that they act as a conduit and will not incur liability** as a tax adviser.

Design and operation considerations

When considering the involvement of sharing/gig economy platforms in educating and informing sharing/gig economy providers on their VAT/GST obligations, tax authorities are encouraged to consider the following specific aspects:

- For sharing/gig economy platforms to be able to carry out their education/communication role, it must be able to rely on information from the tax authorities that is sufficiently focused, clear and up-to-date. Tax authorities need to take account of often limited level of tax literacy of underlying sharing/gig economy providers. Any changes to this information need to be communicated in a timely manner by the tax authorities to the platform, which has to promptly inform their underlying providers.
- The process whereby new sharing/gig economy providers are given access to a digital platform to carry out their sharing/gig economy activities ("onboarding") is the ideal first opportunity to inform sharing/gig economy providers of their VAT/GST obligations. Onboarding is a standard requirement that all sharing/gig economy providers normally must go through.
- It may be important to make the relevant information available in a number of languages (notably in English) especially in sectors where the sharing/gig providers may not necessarily be located in the jurisdiction of taxation (e.g. accommodation).
- Also the tone of communication is likely to have an impact as taxpayers have been found to be generally more receptive to messages written in a simple and positive, friendly manner (c.f. chapter 10 of *Tax Administration 2019 – Comparative Information on OECD and other Advanced and Emerging Economies* (OECD, 2019[6])).
- The involvement of sharing/gig economy platforms in communication with sharing/gig economy providers on their VAT/GST obligations will generally benefit from a close co-operation with tax authorities notably in identifying the appropriate timing of communication, the information needs as they evolve, communication tools and targeted actions. This could for instance include the organisation by platforms of webinars with the tax authorities or webpages with "frequently asked questions" and/or through which a platform's underlying providers can communicate directly with tax authority representatives.

3.3.3. Role(s) performed under a formal co-operation agreement

Formal co-operation agreements are essentially multi-faceted in that they can combine a variety of measures and approaches to involve digital platforms in maximising VAT/GST compliance levels in the sharing/gig economy. They would typically include information sharing (on demand or regular) and education by a digital platform (including using the platform as a conduit to communicate with underlying sharing/gig economy providers on their VAT/GST obligations); alerting the tax authorities of suspected non-compliance or fraud; and responding quickly to notifications by a tax authority where a platform's underlying sharing/gig economy providers are found to be in breach of their VAT/GST obligations. These agreements are concluded on a voluntary basis typically as part of a co-operative compliance approach between tax authority and platform.

Table 3.4. Formal Co-operation Agreements

Opportunities and Challenges - Overview

Opportunities	Challenges
• Could serve as **an intermediary step for other policy tools**, such as a VAT/GST collection or liability role for sharing/gig economy platforms. • May enhance **tax certainty and transparent relationships** and may serve as a proactive approach to addressing material tax risks. • May have a **positive reputational impact for the platforms concerned**, reassuring underlying sharing/gig economy providers and end users as well as compliant competitors.	• **May create a competitive advantage for platforms that do not enter into such an agreement**, which may attract sharing/gig economy providers wishing to avoid or minimize their compliance obligations. Appropriate enforcement action against non-compliance is therefore required (e.g. possible joint and several liability for platforms that permit non-compliance by sharing/gig economy providers on their platform). • **Potential challenges to enforce** the agreement in case the platform fails to deliver. • Digital platforms that facilitate sharing/gig economy supplies in several jurisdictions may need to conclude **multiple agreements** (i.e. one per taxing authority) and, vice versa, tax authorities may have to negotiate multiple similar arrangements with platforms operating in their jurisdiction.

Design and operation considerations

When considering the conclusion of formal co-operation agreements with sharing/gig economy platforms to support VAT/GST compliance by their underlying sharing/gig economy providers, tax authorities are further encouraged to consider the following aspects:

- Close consultation with digital platforms will be required in clearly defining the terms, conditions and timeframe of the agreement. The *Code of Conduct: Co-operation between tax administrations and sharing/gig economy platforms* developed by the Forum on Tax Administration provides for a standardisation of "soft law" approaches to the provision of information by platforms (OECD Forum on Tax Administration, 2020[7]). It may provide an excellent basis for a model on VAT/GST compliance that is acceptable for tax authorities worldwide and may thus reduce complexity for tax authorities from negotiating multiple similar arrangements with platforms operating in their jurisdiction and, vice versa, for platforms that may negotiate such agreements with tax authorities in multiple jurisdictions.
- Jurisdictions may consider making these formal cooperation agreements public to incentivise platforms' participation given the expected positive reputational impact for the platforms concerned.

3.3.4. Information sharing role – Leveraging the OECD model reporting rules

Under an information sharing role, the digital platform is required by law to provide the tax authority with information relevant for VAT/GST compliance and administration without the platform necessarily being liable or having a role in collecting and remitting the VAT/GST due in respect of the activity of underlying sharing/gig economy providers. The below diagram provides an illustrative description of this role.

The platform could be asked to provide the information either upon request or spontaneously (e.g. in case of suspicious activity) and on a regular basis.

Figure 3.2. Information Sharing Role

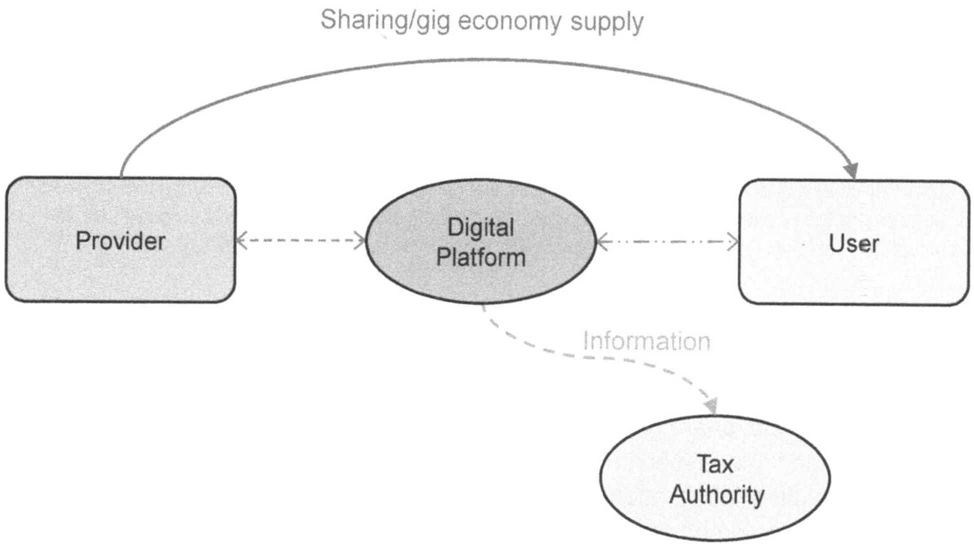

Source: OECD analysis

Table 3.5. Information Sharing Role

Opportunities and challenges – overview

Opportunities	Challenges
• **Potential to leverage the OECD *Model Rules for Reporting by Platforms Operators with respect to Sellers in the Sharing and Gig Economy*[1]** (the OECD Model Reporting Rules (OECD, 2020[3])) so as to avoid duplication of reporting obligations and enhance administrative co-operation. • **The reported information may provide a useful basis for tax authorities** to monitor sharing/gig economy market evolutions within their jurisdiction as well as the possible need for policy response (including per sector). • **May facilitate the detection/prevention of non-compliance** by sharing/gig economy providers including risks of non-registration or under-reporting for VAT/GST purposes. • **May facilitate compliance** via pre-populating VAT/GST returns. • **Enhance the efficiency of the tax administration** by making best use of the data e.g. for advanced risk analysis and enhancing the effectiveness of other measures (e.g. Joint and Several Liability Role for platforms). • **Potential for application to a broader number of platforms** compared to collection/liability roles. • Could assist jurisdictions **in preparing for**	• **Need for adequate human and technical resources** to process the (potentially large) volume of collected information and produce effective analysis in a timely manner. This includes linking and consolidating data from multiple platforms per sharing/gig economy provider (who may often be active on multiple platforms). • **Ensure secure handling of the information collected.** • **Ensure the completeness and reliability of the reported data.** • **Enforce reporting obligations on digital platforms that are outside the taxing jurisdiction** notably in the absence of administrative co-operation agreements between jurisdictions. • **Interaction with other regulatory frameworks, in particular** data protection and privacy legislation and competition law. • **Potential constraints for small and/or start-up platforms to implement** a data transmission mechanism. • **Lack of consistency across jurisdictions in the format and process for data collection** may cause undue compliance burden for platforms faced with reporting obligations in

Opportunities	Challenges
transition towards other regimes for sharing/gig economy platforms, particularly collection/liability roles, by acquiring knowledge about the market and about platforms' and providers' behavior and capabilities.	multiple jurisdictions. This may also make the administrative cooperation among jurisdictions more difficult. The OECD Model Reporting Rules provide a useful basis for enhancing such consistency (OECD, 2020[3]).

Note: [1] The OECD Model Rules define a "Seller" as a Platform user that is registered at any moment during the Reportable period with the platform for the purposes of the provision of Relevant Services. In this light, Sellers can include both individuals and Entities. For the purposes of this report the term "Seller" is used interchangeably with the term "Provider" (OECD, 2020[3]).

Design and operation considerations

Section 3.2.6. above listed a number of overarching principles for the design of information-sharing roles for third parties in the sharing/gig economy, which were not limited to sharing/gig economy platforms. A range of additional aspects are presented below for consideration by tax authorities when designing and implementing information reporting regimes for digital platforms to support VAT/GST compliance in the sharing/gig economy, in particular:

- An information sharing role for sharing/gig economy platforms can be considered as a standalone measure (notably to monitor sharing/gig economy evolutions and/or to monitor compliance by sharing/gig economy providers) or to supplement other roles for digital platforms (notably to complement a joint and several liability regime for platforms that are found to allow non-compliance by their underlying providers). The policy objective(s) of an information sharing regime for sharing/gig economy platforms will largely dictate the type of information that a tax authority will require these platforms to provide. An objective to pre-populate VAT/GST returns is likely to require more detailed information at greater frequency than the objective to monitor providers' compliance with their requirement to register for VAT/GST, which may involve more aggregate data over a longer time period. These objectives, and thus the reporting requirements, may differ depending on the sharing/gig economy sector that is targeted.
- In general terms, it is advised to require platforms to report information which can reasonably be expected to be available to them in the course of their normal business operation, which is proportionally relevant to the tax authority's policy objective(s) and which is not subject to legal limitations for such reporting under data protection or other legal restrictions. It is therefore important that tax authorities gain a proper insight into the data that sharing/gig economy platforms hold on their underlying providers and the activities they facilitate and on their capacity to share that information with tax authorities for VAT/GST compliance purposes, from a technical as well as a legal (e.g. privacy, data protection) perspective.
- The timing of the reporting obligation can have an impact on the quality of the data. Platforms will generally need time to format and run quality checks on the data before reporting them to the tax authorities. Tax authorities may wish to organise the frequency and timing of the reporting requirement so as to provide reasonable time to platforms to process and prepare the data to be transmitted. Tax authorities may further consider separating such information reporting from return filing and other reporting obligations that may involve the same information, as it may be challenging for platforms to comply with different competing reporting and filing obligations at the same time, particularly for small and/or start-up platforms.
- Tax authorities would ideally allow the reported information to be submitted through electronic means so as to allow platform operators to implement an automated reporting process. Early consultation with sharing/gig economy platforms operators when designing an information reporting regime will thus be important for the design of an efficient regime and for its successful operation including a smooth and seamless transmission of data.

- Depending on the ultimate design of the reporting regime, and the associated compliance burden for sharing/gig economy platforms, tax authorities may consider limiting its scope to the platforms that have activities above a certain materiality threshold to avoid risks of disproportionate compliance consequences. Such a threshold could be based on (a combination of) turnover of underlying sharing/gig economy supplies, number of underlying providers and/or volume of transactions facilitated by the platform. Tax authorities could still retain the possibility for information reporting on request in respect of the platforms below such a threshold.
- To further manage the volume of data reported and enhance the efficiency of the reporting regime for sharing/gig economy platforms, tax authorities can exclude the reporting obligation on underlying providers that can be expected to be already known to the tax administration and to be themselves subject to reporting obligations, notably because of the size of their operation. This could for instance apply to taxi/transport firms that also offer their services through a sharing/gig economy platform or a hotel chain that offers short-term accommodation through such a platform. To this end, tax authorities could implement a materiality threshold based on turnover and/or value of transactions above which underlying providers are excluded from the scope of the reporting obligation of the digital platform that facilitates their supplies.
- Tax authorities may consider rules to limit compliance risks in respect of the data reported if they have acted in good faith and made reasonable efforts to ensure the accuracy of these data ("safe harbour" rules). This could include cases where the platform has relied on information provided by tax authorities, notably to ascertain the identity and VAT/GST status of underlying providers and/or users. It can be expected that platforms operate the appropriate due diligence processes in respect of the accuracy and the reliability of the information that they collect in the course of their normal business operation. Tax authorities may wish to align the application of a possible safe harbour rule for digital platforms with the assurance that the appropriate, systems-based, due diligence process is operated.
- As a multitude of digital platforms may be involved in facilitating sharing/gig economy supplies, tax authorities need to provide clear guidance on the reporting requirements for platform(s) in light of their role in the sharing/gig economy process. As a general rule, the platform that is closest to the underlying sharing/gig economy provider will be best placed to report on this provider's activities (typically the platform that has "on boarded" the provider to allow the sharing/gig activity to be carried out). This may in practice lead to a layered reporting, with reporting requirements adjusted to each platform's position in the sharing/gig economy supply chain. In the accommodation sector, for instance, an online travel agent operating its own platform may advertise on another platform in its own name but on behalf of various property owners (as an undisclosed agent; see further under Annex D). The most efficient approach is then for the online travel agent to be required to report on the transactions involving the property owners for which it acts as an undisclosed agent. The platform on which the online travel agent advertises properties in its own name but on behalf of undisclosed other property owners, then reports the transactions of this travel agent (i.e. not the transactions of the underlying property owners).
- Tax authorities will need to ensure that their tax administration has the technological capability and is properly resourced to receive the data reported by sharing/gig economy platforms and to use this information to achieve the intended policy objective(s). A critical aspect to consider in this context is the volume of data that tax authorities expect to receive, which can be significant depending on the sharing/gig economy sector in scope. Reporting at transactional level could, for instance, involve the reporting of thousands of transactions of a relatively small value in certain cases (e.g. the transportation sector). A tax authority may then wish to rather opt for the reporting of, for instance, taxable amounts at aggregated level per underlying sharing/gig

economy provider. It would be unreasonable and inefficient to require information to be reported at a volume and/or level of detail that the tax administration is not capable to process.

- Tax authorities are strongly encouraged to implement a coordinated approach within their tax administration, to ensure that the data collected from digital platforms can be used for different types of taxes (direct and indirect taxes) as appropriate and to minimise risks of duplication of reporting regimes. In this context, jurisdictions are encouraged to leverage on the potential of the OECD Model Reporting Rules to support the implementation of an efficient and coordinated information regime for sharing/gig economy platforms (see further below) (OECD, 2020[3]).
- The OECD Model Reporting Rules are also likely to support consistency across reporting regimes at the international level, including on format and data elements, which is likely to enhance compliance, particularly by platforms that are faced with multi-jurisdictional obligations (OECD, 2020[3]). International consistency is also likely to support the effective international co-operation in tax administration and enforcement. Chapter 4 discusses further potential approaches to support such an effective international co-operation in tax administration and enforcement.

Leveraging the Model Rules for Reporting by Platforms Operators with respect to Sellers in the Sharing and Gig Economy[5] (the OECD Model Reporting Rules) for VAT/GST compliance purposes

The OECD Model Reporting Rules were adopted by the OECD/G20 Inclusive Framework on BEPS in 2020 to assist jurisdictions in implementing a requirement for digital platforms to collect information on the income realised by sharing/gig economy sellers that offer accommodation, transport and personal services and to report the information to tax authorities (OECD, 2020[3]). One of the core objectives of these model rules is to promote international co-operation to ensure that tax administrations have access to information on income earned by sharing/gig economy sellers within their jurisdictions, including from platforms that are located in other jurisdictions. To achieve this, the rules provide that platform operators report information to the tax authorities of the jurisdiction in which these operators are resident; and that this information is exchanged automatically and annually by the residence jurisdiction of the platform operator with the jurisdictions of residence of the sellers - and, with respect to transactions involving the rental of immovable property, the jurisdictions in which such immovable property is located.

The OECD Model Reporting Rules promote standardisation of reporting rules between jurisdictions in order to help platforms comply with reporting obligations across different jurisdictions, by allowing them to follow largely similar processes for gathering and reporting information on the transactions and identity of the platform sellers (OECD, 2020[3]). Annex C to this report provides further detailed information on the key features of the OECD Model Reporting Rules (OECD, 2020[3]).

The OECD Model Reporting Rules have been designed primarily to facilitate and enhance compliance by sharing/gig economy providers with their direct tax obligations (OECD, 2020[3]). They recognise explicitly, however, that the information reported and exchanged under these rules is likely to be relevant for VAT/GST compliance purposes also. The information reported under the OECD Model Reporting Rules will include the consideration received by sharing/gig economy providers, the types/number of services provided and the underlying provider's tax identification data (OECD, 2020[3]). This information is likely to be relevant for VAT/GST compliance purposes in the jurisdiction receiving the information under the Model Reporting Rules (OECD, 2020[3]). Depending on the type of services and the applicable rules for determining their VAT/GST place of taxation, the tax authorities may benefit from the information received under the Model Reporting Rules (OECD, 2020[3]) for VAT/GST compliance purposes as follows:

- In general, tax authorities in the jurisdiction where a sharing/gig economy provider is established, will be able to use the information received under the Model Reporting Rules to verify this provider's compliance with its VAT/GST registration obligation (and associated obligations such as reporting, application of simplification regimes, etc.) (OECD, 2020[3]);
- Where a tax authority receives information on a sharing/gig economy provider in its jurisdiction in respect of supplies that are subject to VAT/GST in this jurisdiction, the tax administration will be able to use these data to monitor and pursue compliance by this provider with all the associated VAT/GST obligations, including the provider's obligation to register, report and remit the VAT/GST. This will typically apply to supplies of services for which the VAT/GST place of taxation is determined by reference to their place of performance or by reference to the location of the supplier (typically "on-the-spot" services as described in Guideline 3.5. of the *International VAT/GST Guidelines* (OECD, 2017[4])). This is important in the sharing/gig economy context, as these will often involve such "on-the-spot" services that will be subject to VAT/GST in the jurisdiction where the sharing/gig economy provider is established, such as local transportation and delivery services and personal services.
- Where information is received by a tax authority relating to services connected with immovable property that is located in this tax authority's jurisdiction, this tax administration will be able to use this information to monitor compliance with all the VAT/GST obligations in respect of these services. Indeed, such services will in general be subject to VAT/GST in the jurisdiction where the relevant immovable property is located (see Guideline 3.8. of the *International VAT/GST Guidelines* (OECD, 2017[4])). This information will be particularly useful to monitor and pursue compliance with VAT/GST obligations in the accommodation (short-term rental) sector of the sharing/gig economy.

It is thus clear that the information that will be exchanged under the OECD Model Reporting Rules will be of significant use for authorities to enhance VAT/GST compliance in key sectors of the sharing/gig economy, including the sectors of transportation, personal services and accommodation (OECD, 2020[3]). It is important that tax authorities ensure that the information exchanged under these rules is used effectively to address their VAT/GST reporting needs at the national level as well as to support the international VAT/GST cooperation in this context. This will notably minimise risks of uncoordinated proliferation of reporting requirements that would have an adverse impact on the efficiency and costs of tax administration and compliance for both tax administrations and economic operators.

Where the information exchanged under these Model Reporting Rules (OECD, 2020[3]) is intended to be used for purposes other than the administration of direct taxes by the receiving tax administration, jurisdictions should ensure that the information is shared and used in compliance with the relevant confidentiality and appropriate use provisions of the underlying international exchange instrument, such as Article 22 of the *Multilateral Convention on Mutual Administrative Assistance in Tax Matters* (OECD/Council of Europe, 2011[8]).

While the information covered by the Model Reporting Rules will thus be valuable for VAT/GST compliance purposes in respect of an important range of sharing/gig economy supplies, including in sectors that are likely to need the most urgent attention given their size and further growth potential, it is recognised that these rules may not satisfy all VAT/GST needs (OECD, 2020[3]). This may for instance be the case for services that are subject to VAT/GST in another jurisdiction than the jurisdiction where the relevant provider or the relevant immovable property is located. Moreover the annual frequency of information exchange may not satisfy all needs for VAT/GST reporting (given the transactional nature of the tax and the higher frequency of VAT/GST reporting and payment obligations). Against this background, it is recognised that a further extension of reporting requirements for VAT/GST purposes may be necessary over time. It is important to note in this context that the Model Reporting Rules acknowledge that reporting on other types of transactions is likely to become relevant in the future (OECD, 2020[3]). This could for instance include types of services that are not yet included in its scope such as the rental of moveable assets and peer-to-peer lending. The Model Reporting Rules anticipate that the possible further development and expansion of these rules will take due account of VAT/GST compliance needs, notably in determining the scope of reporting and the reporting flows (OECD, 2020[3]).

The Model Reporting Rules do not seek to dictate jurisdictions to introduce them (OECD, 2020[3]). They rather encourage jurisdictions that wish to introduce reporting rules aimed at the sharing/gig economy, to do so in a manner that is consistent with the Model Reporting Rules (OECD, 2020[3]). This is expected to enhance consistency of reporting regimes across jurisdictions, which will promote and facilitate international co-operation between tax administrations including to support VAT/GST compliance in the sharing/gig economy. By supporting the international exchange of information, the Model Reporting Rules are likely to offer the most powerful tool for tax authorities to gather information on supplies and providers that are subject to VAT/GST in their jurisdiction from non-resident sharing/gig economy platforms (OECD, 2020[3]).

This is an important advantage that the Model Reporting Rules are likely to have over purely domestic reporting regimes for VAT/GST purposes, as it may be challenging to enforce such reporting requirements against non-resident platform operators (OECD, 2020[3]). On the other hand, platforms facilitating transactions in multiple jurisdictions may be confronted with a wide set of diverging domestic reporting requirements in the absence of coordination, which may lead to increased costs, potentially harmful barriers to the business development and a negative effect on compliance and data quality.

Overall, international consistency promoted by the Model Reporting Rules is thus expected to facilitate compliance, lower compliance costs and administrative burdens and improve the effectiveness of VAT/GST systems recognising in particular that digital platforms are likely to be faced with multi-jurisdictional obligations (OECD, 2020[3]).

Jurisdictions are thus strongly encouraged to leverage, as appropriate, the potential of the Model Reporting Rules to monitor and enhance VAT/GST compliance in the sharing/gig economy (OECD, 2020[3]).

These Model Reporting Rules could more generally provide the appropriate basis for a future expansion of information reporting and exchange in the area of VAT/GST (OECD, 2020[3]).

3.3.5. Joint and several liability regime (JSL)

Under a Joint and Several Liability regime, if the underlying sharing/gig economy provider is not VAT/GST compliant, the tax authorities have the possibility to declare the platform facilitating the sharing/gig economy supply jointly and severally liable for the VAT/GST due. The underlying provider remains itself VAT/GST liable. Such a regime requires that the sharing/gig economy activities are within the scope of VAT/GST in line with the national legislation of the taxing jurisdiction and that the sharing/gig economy provider is liable to register, collect and pay VAT/GST on the supplies performed. Such a regime could operate under two main variations which are not mutually exclusive. In particular:

- ***Under Variation 1 of the JSL regime,*** the platform is held jointly and severally liable for the **future undeclared VAT/GST** on the underlying sharing/gig economy providers, once the tax authority has spotted cases of non-compliance, has reported these cases to the digital platform and the latter did not take appropriate action within a specified period. Such action by the digital platform typically consists of securing compliance from the underlying provider or removing the provider from its platform. This variation can in principle be implemented without the requirement for the tax authority to prove that the digital platform knew that the underlying provider was not compliant.
- ***Under Variation 2 of the JSL regime,*** the sharing/gig economy platform may be held jointly and severally liable **for the past undeclared VAT/GST for the underlying provider** when the

digital platform should have had a reasonable expectation based on the underlying provider's activities on the platform that the provider should be registered for VAT/GST but has not. It is for the taxing jurisdiction to determine when such a reasonable expectation exists.

Such a regime does not necessarily ensure that any lost VAT/GST is collected. For example, under Variation 1, the platform would have the possibility to escape the JSL by taking the necessary safeguard actions towards the provider (i.e. remove it from the platform). Indeed, in such case the tax authorities would have no other option than to pursue the collection of the VAT/GST due form the underlying provider. JSL could be considered as a tool to encourage and enforce compliance by underlying sharing/gig economy providers, by incentivizing sharing/gig economy platforms to pursue such compliance from the providers that use their platform (and/or by creating disincentives for platforms against tolerate non-compliance by providers on their platform).

The following diagram provides an illustrative description of this regime.

Figure 3.3. Joint and Several Liability Role

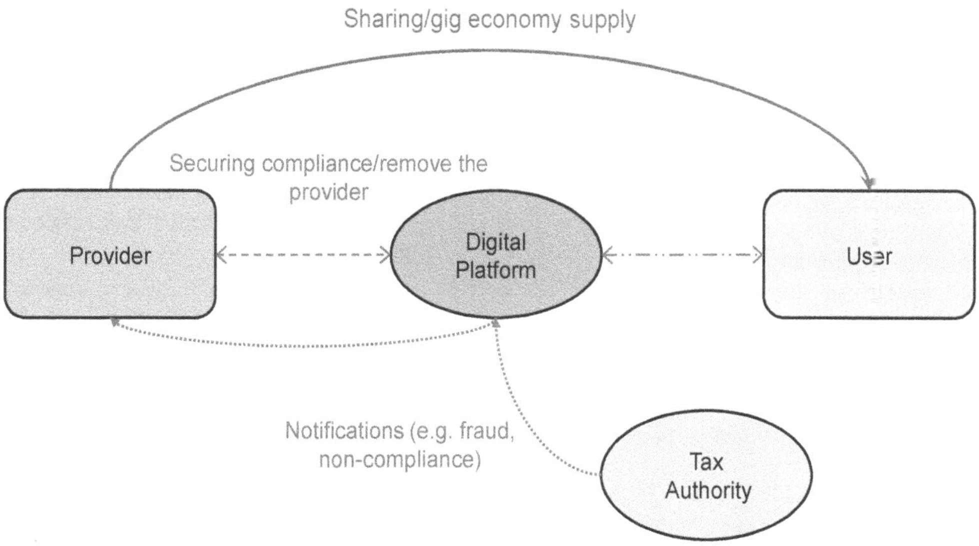

Source: OECD analysis

Table 3.6. Joint and Several Liability Regime

Opportunities and Challenges - Overview

Opportunities	Challenges
• It **provides a mechanism to enforce compliance on non-compliant underlying providers** notably by requiring platforms to block non-compliant underlying providers from operating on them. • **May have a significant preventive effect as sharing/gig economy** providers will not want to be moved from the platforms. • It builds on the assumption that it is **in the interest of platforms to ensure a level playing field for all of their providers** and to remove "bad actors"; and that the digital platforms will be compliant. • **Leverage the importance of reputation and trust in the sharing/gig economy** both for platforms and providers. It is reasonable to expect that the measure will still have a detrimental impact on providers even if they manage to register again with a platform for instance by using a different identity (as the provider will lose its trusted profile). • Enhance the effectiveness of other roles. A JSL can notably be used as **a fallback to incentivize compliance with an information sharing obligation**.	• Under JSL variation 1, the tax authorities need to first detect non-compliance and provide a list of the non-compliant **providers** to the platform(s) on which these providers operate, which **may be beyond a tax administration's current capacity**. Under JSL variation 2, the tax authorities will need to prove additionally that the platform operator was reasonably aware that the sharing/gig economy provider was not complying with its tax obligations. • An important limitation to the effectiveness of JSL variation 2 is that a digital platform may not always know with certainty whether an underlying provider may be subject to VAT/GST registration and compliance in a jurisdiction that applies a registration or collection threshold. **It is typical for sharing/gig economy providers to operate across multiple platforms.** While these providers' activity may remain below the relevant threshold on each of these platforms, its aggregated activity may be above the threshold. • A complicating factor **in the accommodation sector** of the sharing/gig economy is that **the identity of the underlying provider may not always be readily available** to the facilitating platform (see also in Annex D). This is for instance the case where a property is managed and advertised by a professional agent on behalf of its owner. Even where the information on the underlying provider is known to the platform, it may connect the relevant turnover to the professional agent rather than to the underlying provider (owner or otherwise). Similar issues may apply to renters that may use the platforms to raise additional income, sometimes without the knowledge or approval of the owner of the property. Non-compliant providers that are removed from a platform under a JSL obligation for the platform, **may register again** on the same or another platform using a different identity. This risk may be limited in practice. In the accommodation sector, the data on the location of the property may serve as a filter to avoid re-registration of the same property. Similarly, in the transportation sector, a driver's driving license might be used to limit blocked drivers from reregistering.

Design and operation considerations

When considering a joint and several liability role for digital platforms in enhancing VAT/GST compliance by underlying sharing/gig economy providers, tax authorities are encouraged to take account of the following additional aspects:

- It is critical that JSL regimes for sharing/gig economy platforms are enforced across the sharing/gig economy as a whole so as to avoid that non-compliant providers simply continue their activity on other platforms. If a supplier is found to be non-compliant, then all the platforms in which it is active need to be notified.
- A JSL regime needs to ensure that reasonable time is available for well-intentioned sharing /gig economy providers to regularise their VAT/GST position if needed, i.e. for providers to register for VAT/GST purposes when they are required to do so and for the sharing/gig platforms to remove/block non-compliant providers from their platform. JSL regimes thus notably need to be consistent with the performance of a jurisdiction's VAT/GST registration process for sharing/gig economy providers (see also Section 3.2.3). Under Variation 1 it may be appropriate to allow reasonable time to the platform to first reach out to providers that have been found to be non-compliant and, if non-compliance has indeed been established, then additionally to ensure that these underlying suppliers complete the registration and provide the VAT/GST number to the platform.
- Under Variation 1, electronic means of communication are preferable to paper-based communication in notifying the platforms of underlying providers' non-compliance, particularly for non-resident platforms. It would also be practically efficient to establish a contact point within each platform for communication with tax authorities.
- Proportionality of JSL regimes needs to be safeguarded. In particular under Variation 2, it would be disproportionate to hold a platform unconditionally liable for unpaid VAT/GST where it cannot reasonably be expected to be in position to be aware of the non-compliance, e.g. where an underlying provider is registered but underreports its activity in its VAT/GST return or where a provider has exceeded a registration threshold through its activities via another platform. A safe harbour provision could be considered to protect a platform against liability under a JSL regime if it can satisfy the tax authorities that it has taken all reasonable measures to avoid the non-compliance of underlying providers. Tax authorities could for instance impose a number of predetermined checks for platforms to undertake and limit joint and several liability to cases where the provider does not meet the requirements set by those checks.
- A JSL will likely need to be combined with an information sharing obligation on platforms to be effective, notably as underlying providers are likely to operate via more than one platform. Indeed, sharing/gig economy providers often operate across multiple platforms making it difficult for tax authorities and platforms to know if and when they have exceeded a registration threshold where applicable. Tax authorities will be in a better position to monitor sharing/gig economy providers' compliance in this respect if platforms share information on these underlying providers with the tax authorities.

3.3.6. Full liability regime (FLR)

Under the full VAT/GST liability regime (FLR), the digital platform is designated by law as the supplier for VAT/GST liability purposes. Under this regime the digital platform is solely and fully liable for assessing, collecting and remitting the VAT/GST on the sharing/gig economy activity that goes through the platform, to the tax authorities in the jurisdiction of taxation, in line with the VAT/GST legislation of that jurisdiction. This liability regime is limited to VAT/GST obligations only. It does not affect any other liability aspects for digital platforms beyond the VAT/GST.

The underlying sharing/gig economy provider is in principle relieved from any VAT/GST liability on the supply to its customer/user. In order to avoid a break in the staged collection chain, the FLR may treat the digital platform as having received the supply from the underlying provider and having supplied it onwards to the customer/user.

Depending on the policy objective and national specifics, potential variations of the FLR could include the following:

- **Variation 1**: the FLR applies only in cases where the underlying supplier is regarded as a taxable person for VAT/GST purposes under national law.
- **Variation 2**: the FLR applies irrespective of the status of the underlying supplier for VAT/GST purposes under national law.

The following diagram provides an illustrative description of the role.

Figure 3.4. Full Liability Regime

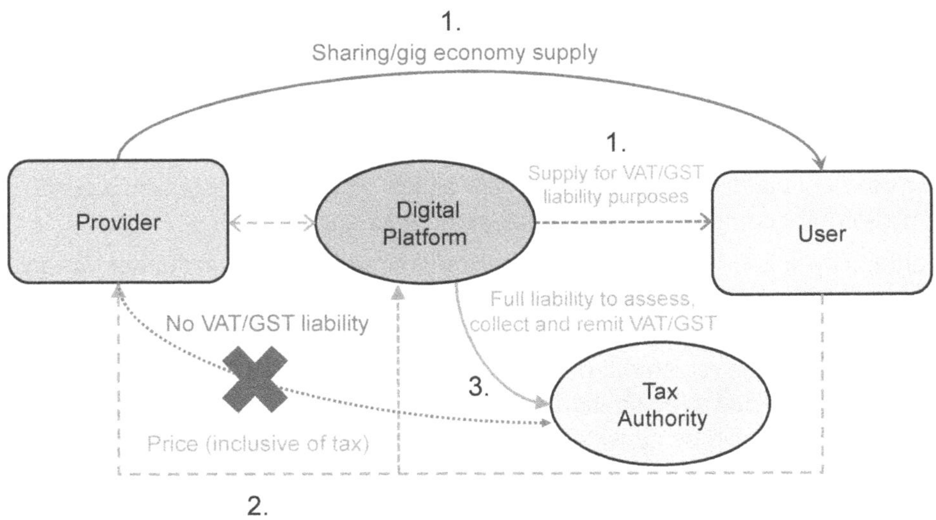

Note: the sequence of numbers assigned in the diagram is for identification only. It is not intended to indicate the timing of a specific step in chronological order.
Source: OECD analysis.

Table 3.7. Full liability regime

Opportunities and Challenges – Overview

Opportunities	Challenges
• **Significant reduction of costs and of revenue and compliance risks for VAT/GST administration.** Tax authorities' efforts to administer, police and collect the VAT/GST on the ever-increasing volumes of sharing/gig activities can be focused on a relatively limited number of platforms that facilitate large shares of the sharing/gig economy instead of on the continuously growing number of new and often small sharing/gig economy providers. This includes the reduction of administrative burden and risk associated with the recovery of large number of small VAT/GST debts. • **May well be the only feasible option for tax authorities with limited administrative capacity** to levy VAT/GST on sharing/gig	• **Sharing/gig economy providers and supplies that were not subject to VAT/GST may become subject to VAT/GST purely as a consequence of the application of a FLR.** This would result from the fact that the determination of VAT/GST status and the application of VAT/GST registration and/or collection thresholds occur at the level of the FLR platform rather than at the level of the individual sharing/gig economy provider. Under FLR Variation 1, supplies that would normally not incur VAT/GST below a provider's VAT/GST registration or collection threshold may thus become subject to VAT/GST. In addition, under FLR Variation 2, supplies by private individuals that are normally outside the VAT/GST scope (including C2C) may become subject to VAT/GST.

Opportunities	Challenges
economy activities in its jurisdiction. • **Likely to enhance overall VAT/GST compliance levels,** as sharing/gig economies platforms, particularly the largest ones, are best placed to comply. They are most likely to have access to the necessary resources and information and have a reputational incentive to comply. • **Potential to facilitate compliance for underlying sharing/gig economy providers subject to VAT/GST,** in particular in calculating and remitting the tax. The underlying provider may still need to comply with VAT/GST reporting obligations, including keeping records to demonstrate that supplies were made through the platform that has collected and remitted the VAT/GST. • **Potential to protect and/or broaden the tax base by formalizing (new) activities** that may otherwise remain in the informal economy, as sharing/gig economy providers may lack the capacity and/or incentives to comply with their tax and other regulatory obligations (municipal, sanitary, etc.) • **Potential to reduce the distortive impact of VAT/GST non-compliance** for compliant actors.	This may have a significant negative effect on the earnings and/or profit margins of sharing/gig economy providers. It may also increase the number of VAT/GST taxpayers, which could be eligible for input VAT/GST deduction in the absence of targeted simplification measures. It could also create a disincentive for potentially affected categories of sharing/gig economy providers to use FLR platforms and lead to competitive distortion for these platforms. Tax authorities are advised to carefully assess these consequences, which are likely to differ from sector to sector. • **Particular challenges could arise for tax authorities from managing the deduction of input VAT/GST for sharing/gig economy providers** whose supplies become subject to VAT/GST as a result of the application of the FLR (see previous bullet). This could for instance include drivers claiming deduction of input VAT/GST on their vehicle and fuel costs. This can create considerable administrative burden and compliance risks (including in respect of input-VAT/GST deduction on assets used for business and private purposes) and reduce the net revenue from the application of the FLR considerably. A simplification measure (e.g. lump sum input VAT/GST credit) could be considered to manage this risk. • **Enforcement risks may increase from moving VAT/GST liability from a taxpayer (i.e. the sharing/gig provider) with a presence in the taxing jurisdiction to a platform that may be outside the taxing jurisdiction. Sharing/gig economy providers are often likely to have a presence in the taxing jurisdiction.** This is notably the case in the important accommodation and transportation sectors of the sharing/gig economy, which are (respectively) generally subject to VAT/GST in the jurisdiction where the immovable property is situated and where transport takes place. In theory, moving VAT/GST liability for these supplies to a non-resident platform may increases enforcement risks. These risks may also involve considerable amounts per platform. In practice, however, these platforms have significant incentives to comply including reputational and regulatory (in particular for publicly listed platform operators). • **Additional complexity may arise from moving VAT/GST compliance processes from VAT/GST providers that already comply and pay the VAT/GST to a platform** (notably in a "platform on platform" business model – see in Annex D). To reduce such risks, consideration could be given to

Opportunities	Challenges
	limit the scope of a FLR to underlying sharing/gig economy providers below a certain threshold (recognising that this may have its own complexities for platforms, including of having to monitor providers' thresholds). • **Interaction of the deemed supply with place of taxation rules may need further consideration in cases of cross-border supplies.** This may be less relevant for the accommodation services where, contrary to the transportation, there are already internationally agreed guidelines with respect to the determination of the taxing jurisdiction for consumption purposes (*International VAT/GST Guidelines*, Guideline 3.8. (OECD, 2017[4])). • Not all platforms that may meet the criteria to be enlisted under a FLR may reasonably be **in a position to comply with the FLR, particularly start-ups and small platforms.** • **It may be challenging for platforms facilitating mixed or bundled services to determine the correct VAT/GST treatment of these services. For instance** a travel package including accommodation, transportation, meals, excursions, etc.

Design and operation considerations

The table above shows that a full liability regime may have great potential for tax authorities in facilitating the efficient application of VAT/GST to sharing/gig economy activities and in enhancing overall VAT/GST compliance levels in this context. It may come, however, with a number of challenges that may be considerable depending on the design of the regime and the sector to which it applies (its size, complexity, cross-border nature, etc.). It will be important for tax authorities to pursue the appropriate balance between these challenges and opportunities, possible by accompanying the FLR with simplification measures to limit the VAT/GST compliance aspects for underlying sharing/gig economy suppliers (see below and further detail in Section 3.2.2 above). In addition to what has been set out above, tax authorities are encouraged to consider the following aspects:

- When considering whether a sharing/gig economy platform is capable to comply with a FLR, tax authorities are advised to essentially consider the two following core aspects:
  - Whether the sharing/gig economy platform has access to sufficient and accurate information to make the appropriate VAT/GST determination. In particular, the platform will need the appropriate information to determine core elements in a reliable manner: the identity and (under Variation 1) the status of its underlying sharing/gig economy providers; the nature of the supply; its value; and its VAT/GST treatment (including place of taxation, possible exemption, rate.). This VAT/GST treatment may not always be that straightforward and may require access to specific information elements. For example in the accommodation sector, supplies may be treated differently depending on whether they include the leasing of a furnished or unfurnished apartment with or without additional (hotel-type) services. Similarly in the transportation sector the VAT/GST treatment may differ depending on whether it involves a ride-sourcing service against a fee or ride-sharing/car-pooling under a cost sharing arrangement (e.g. passengers contribute in the estimated

costs of the trip to the driver) (see further discussion on available information elements in Annex D).

- Whether the sharing/gig economy platform has the means (ability) to collect the VAT/GST due on the sharing/gig economy supply (see different payment models in Annex D). A platform can be reasonably expected to have the means (ability) to collect the VAT/GST due on the sharing/gig economy supply it facilitates when it is involved in the electronic payment process for these supplies. As highlighted in chapter 1 of this report, the use of electronic (often online) payment is one of the typical features of the sharing/gig economy. Challenges may arise where payments are made in cash, which may still be the case in the transportation sector, particularly in developing economies). In such cases, tax authorities will need to give due consideration to a solution that limits financial risks and compliance burdens for platforms from having to potentially (pre)finance VAT/GST for underlying providers that are remunerated by their customers in cash.

- The functions performed by a sharing/gig economy platform in the normal course of its business can serve as useful indicators of this platform's capability to comply with the FLR, in light of the two core aspects outlined above. Particularly useful (non-exhaustive) indicators include the following:
  - the level of control that the platform exercises in setting the terms and conditions of the supply (e.g. high degree of standardisation of the service and an extended knowledge of the sharing/gig economy suppliers' activities);
  - the control over the payment for the sharing/gig economy supply (directly or indirectly);
  - the extent in which the platform presents itself as the supplier to the consumer (the "consumer-facing" approach), the degree in which the platform provides guarantees the quality of the services, security protection, refund in case of cancellation unsatisfactory service...

  In contrast, platforms that merely list or advertise services; or only process payments; or only provide the technical means or capacity to carry data (e.g. provide internet network capacity via cable, satellite etc.; data storage capacity etc.) are unlikely to be in a position to comply with a full liability regime and can thus be excluded from its scope. The list of functions in the Annex A. of the 2019 Digital Platforms report are of equal relevance for the application of FLR on platforms facilitating sharing/gig economy supplies (see in Annex E to this report) (OECD, 2019[1]). In any case, a FLR needs to be designed as future proof and as flexible as possible given the continuous evolution of the sharing/gig economy and the digital platforms economy more generally, which may impact platforms' eligibility for such a regime.

- To enhance and facilitate compliance by non-resident platforms, it is advised to operate a simplified registration regime as recommended by the *International VAT/GST Guidelines* (OECD, 2017[4]) and for these platforms to comply with the VAT/GST obligations under a full liability regime. Where compliance procedures are too complex, their application for non-resident digital platforms may lead to non-compliance or to certain digital platforms declining to operate in certain jurisdictions. The challenges of enforcing obligations on platforms that are not located in the taxing jurisdiction are further discussed under Chapter 4.

- In order to avoid a break in the staged collection chain, the FLR may treat the sharing/gig economy platform as having received the supply from the underlying provider and having supplied it onwards to the customer/user. In this context the taxing jurisdiction may wish to treat this supply as zero-rated and/or subject to reduced VAT/GST compliance burden for both providers and platforms, to reduce revenue risks for tax authorities (from generating recoverable VAT/GST for digital platforms that needs to be collected from the underlying providers) and reduce cash-flow costs for platforms (of having to pay VAT/GST to their underlying providers and subsequently recover it via their VAT/GST return).

- To minimize the administrative burden and compliance risks from input VAT/GST deduction claims by underlying sharing/gig economy providers, careful consideration could be given to complementing the FLR with a simplification measure for the underlying providers such as a presumptive or flat rate tax scheme or a VAT/GST input tax credit scheme through the provider's income tax return (see further analysis under Section 3.2.2. above).
- Zero-rating of the fees charged by the digital platform to its underlying sharing/gig economy providers, depending on the business model that is used, could be considered to further reduce the possible amounts of deductible input VAT/GST for the providers (and further simplify their VAT/GST compliance), to reduce cash-flow costs for these underlying providers and to avoid double taxation in case these fees (and the VAT/GST on these fees) would be embedded in the final price of the sharing/gig economy supply on which VAT/GST is collected by the platform.
- A full liability regime for sharing/gig economy platforms requires simple and straightforward rules with clear definitions of the VAT/GST obligations of the platforms and of the underlying providers. This includes clear rules on the VAT/GST status of the relationship between the underlying provider and the digital platform and the associated compliance obligations (invoicing, reporting, etc.).
- FLR also requires careful consideration of the design and operation of thresholds (if any), in particular whether they apply at the level of the platform or of the underling provider and how they are calculated (does the platform have the capacity and information to monitor its underlying providers' thresholds?). Policy decisions on this aspect are likely to have significant impact on revenue, compliance and administration.
- Consideration may need to be given to the interaction between the FLR and other sector-specific VAT/GST regimes such as tourist operator margin schemes.
- Digital platforms are likely to require certainty that the application of a FLR remains limited to VAT/GST and that it does not influence treatment in other areas, such as for inst Key fance labour law.

3.3.7. Collection role/withholding role

Under a collection/withholding regime, the platform acts as a third-party service provider or on behalf of the underlying sharing/gig economy provider to calculate, collect and remit the VAT/GST owed. The below diagram provides an illustrative description of the role.

Key features

- The platform incurs no other VAT/GST liability than the responsibility to collect/withhold the VAT/GST due on the underlying sharing/gig economy supply and pass it on to the tax authorities in the jurisdiction of taxation. The underlying sharing/gig economy provider remains liable for the VAT/GST towards the tax authorities.
- Depending on the design, the underlying provider may still need to fulfil its VAT/GST reporting obligations (i.e. the only relief is the payment of the VAT/GST via the platform).
- Such a regime could be designed on a voluntary basis (under an agreement between the underlying supplier and the platform) or on a mandatory basis (imposed by law).

Figure 3.5. Collection Role/Withholding Role

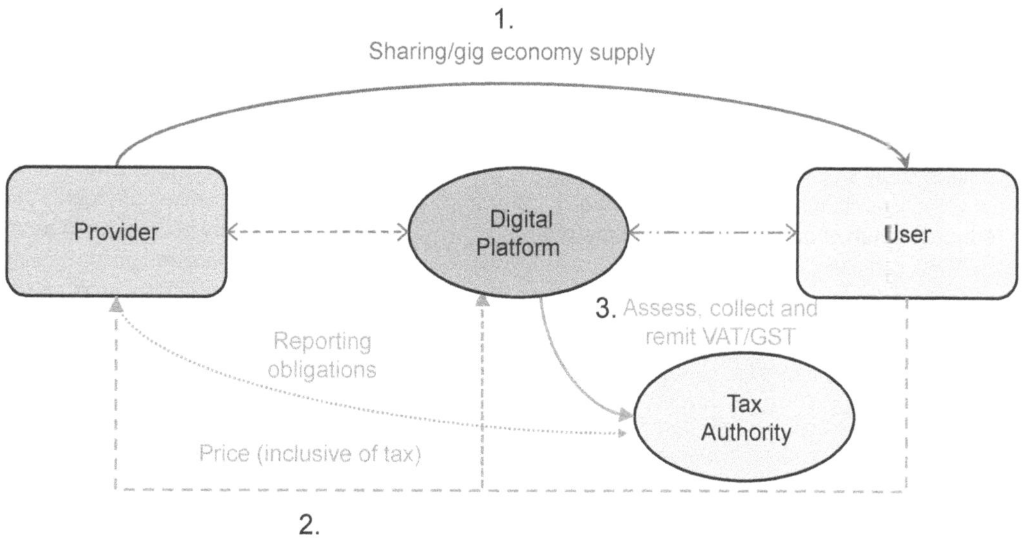

Note: the sequence of numbers assigned in the diagram is for identification only. It is not intended to indicate the timing of a specific step in chronological order.
Source: OECD analysis

Table 3.8. Collection Role/Withholding Role

Opportunities and Challenges - Overview

Opportunities	Challenges
• **May facilitate VAT/GST compliance considerably for sharing/gig economy providers with limited capacity**, by relieving them from the core responsibility to calculate, collect and remit the VAT/GST on their activities to the tax authorities. The underlying provider may however still need to fulfil VAT/GST reporting obligations (e.g. for input VAT/GST deduction purposes). • **Platforms may offer a VAT/GST collection/withholding role as part of their service offering** to their underlying sharing/gig economy providers without incurring the risk of full VAT/GST liability. • **Likely to enhance overall compliance levels** as the platforms are generally best placed to ensure a correct VAT/GST collection on the sharing/gig economy supplies they facilitate (in terms of information, resources and technological capacity as well as reputational incentive). • **Potential to protect and/or broaden the VAT/GST base** by ensuring the proper collection of VAT/GST on activities that may have otherwise remained in the informal economy. Without assistance from the platforms,	• Tax authorities will **still have to administer and monitor the thousands of underlying sharing/gig economy providers** in respect of their overall VAT/GST compliance, including their filing and reporting obligations (as appropriate). • **Where VAT/GST rules for the underlying sharing/gig supplies are complex, it may be particularly challenging** for platforms to carry out a collection/ withholding role. Where a registration/collection threshold applies for underlying sharing/gig economy providers, its application may difficult for any platform to assess in isolation as providers may operate via various platforms. Complexity may also arise from the application of multiple VAT/GST rates and/or exemptions. • For underlying sharing/gig economy providers that have a right to deduct input VAT/GST under normal rules, **the collection/withholding of VAT/GST via the platform can lead to a structural input VAT/GST credit position.** This applies in particular where input VAT/GST remains deductible by the underlying provider under normal VAT/GST rules, as there may be

Opportunities	Challenges
sharing/gig economy providers may often lack the capacity and the incentive to formalize their activity and comply with their tax and other regulatory obligations (municipal, sanitary, etc.) • By limiting the scope for VAT/GST non-compliance by sharing/gig economy suppliers, the collection/withholding regime is **likely to reduce the risk of competitive distortion** with VAT/GST compliant actors.	no or insufficient output VAT/GST against which deductible input VAT/GST can be credited. This can create considerable cash-flow pressure for underlying providers and complexity for VAT/GST administration of having process potentially large numbers of small refund claims from sharing/gig economy providers. These challenges may vary from sector to sector, and be more limited where underlying providers are less likely to incur significant amounts of deductible input VAT/GST (e.g. activities that rely primarily on labor). The application of measures to simplify input VAT/GST deduction or underlying providers can further reduce the challenges in this context (see Section 3.2.2 above). • While sharing/gig economy platforms can generally be expected to comply with their obligations under a VAT/GST collection/withholding regime (particularly the large, established operators), **enforcement challenges could arise in respect of non-resident platforms.** This may be particularly challenging in respect of start-ups and smaller, less established platforms. Especially where this regime is not mandatory, administrative co-operation and exchange of information between the taxing jurisdiction and the jurisdiction where the platform is located may be challenging to the extent that there is no definite legal status (VAT/GST liability) for the platform that is subject to the collection/withholding role. • **Fraud by underlying sharing/gig providers cannot be totally excluded as the platforms' responsibility** is merely to collect/withhold the VAT/GST based on the information at its disposal.

Design and operation considerations

Tax authorities may wish to consider the following additional policy and operational aspects when designing a possible collection/withholding regime for sharing/gig economy platforms to support VAT/GST compliance by sharing/gig economy providers:

- A collection/withholding regime operates as a lighter version of a full liability role, in that the platform collects/withholds the VAT/GST due on sharing/gig economy supplies that it facilitates and remits it to the tax authorities without incurring wider VAT/GST liability towards the tax authorities. The underlying sharing/gig economy provider remains ultimately liable to the tax authorities for the VAT/GST on its supplies. There is thus no need to treat the platform as the supplier of the underlying sharing/gig economy supplies (as under the full-liability regime), nor to treat the digital platform as having received the supply from the underlying sharing/gig economy provider and having supplied in onwards to the customer/user. However, a collection/withholding role does involve a number of VAT/GST obligations and possible compliance risks for platforms, which are particularly important to consider when designing the legal framework for such a regime. In this context, the design and operation considerations discussed under the full liability role (see Section 3.3.6) are of equal relevance for the design of a collection/withholding role. In particular, the following two core conditions are critical for a successful operation of both regimes:

- The eligible platform needs to hold or have access to sufficient and accurate information as required to make the appropriate VAT/GST determination in respect of the underlying VAT/GST supply (status of underlying provider and customer/user, nature of the supply, price, applicable VAT/GST rate, place of taxation…);
- The platform must have the means (the ability) to collect/withhold the VAT/GST due on the sharing/gig economy supply it facilitates. This means, in principle, that the platform should be involved in some way (directly or indirectly) in the payment for the underlying supply by the customer/user or be reasonably able to ensure such involvement.

- The underlying sharing/gig economy providers remain ultimately liable for the VAT/GST due on their supplies, even though it is collected/withheld and remitted to the tax authorities by the platform that facilitates these supplies. These underlying providers therefore need to be informed of the amounts of VAT/GST collected/withheld and paid by the platform to the tax authorities on their behalf, to fulfil their own reporting obligations. This could involve a regular recapitulative statement with the VAT/GST amounts collected/withheld and remitted, to be issued by the platform to the underlying provider. This will need to be taken into account by tax authorities when considering the filing and reporting regime for underlying sharing/gig economy providers, so as to ensure that they have the means and sufficient time to receive and process the data from the platform. Simplification measures for sharing/gig economy providers to limit their filing and reporting requirements could be helpful in addressing this challenge (see notably Section 3.2.3.).
- In light of the above, tax authorities need to be aware that a requirement to remit the VAT/GST for each underlying provider to the tax authorities separately and the associated reporting (connecting the amounts remitted to each underlying provider individually) may be challenging for sharing/gig economy platforms, particularly start-ups and smaller platforms and/or platforms that face collection/withholding obligations in multiple jurisdictions.
- Safe-harbour rules may need to be considered to protect both platforms and underlying providers from liability for potential errors made in good faith and despite reasonable efforts. This could for instance apply to a digital platform relying on information that turned out to be incorrect despite reasonable efforts made to verify its validity. Or to an underlying provider for errors that were made by the platform despite having provided correct and timely information.

References

Milanez, A. and B. Bratta (2019), "Taxation and the future of work: How tax systems influence choice of employment form", *OECD Taxation Working Papers*, No. 41, OECD Publishing, Paris, https://dx.doi.org/10.1787/20f7164a-en. [10]

OECD (2020), *Model Rules for Reporting by Platform Operators with respect to Sellers in the Sharing and Gig Economy*, OECD , Paris, https://www.oecd.org/tax/exchange-of-tax-information/model-rules-for-reporting-by-platform-operators-with-respect-to-sellers-in-the-sharing-and-gig-economy.htm (accessed on 25 February 2021). [3]

OECD (2019), *Implementing Online Cash Registers: Benefits, Considerations and Guidance*, OECD , Paris, http://www.oecd.org/ctp/implementing-online-cash-registers-benefits-considerations-and-guidance.htm (accessed on 25 February 2021). [2]

OECD (2019), *Tax Administration 2019: Comparative Information on OECD and other Advanced and Emerging Economies*, OECD Publishing, Paris, https://dx.doi.org/10.1787/74d162b6-en. [6]

OECD (2019), *The Role of Digital Platforms in the Collection of VAT/GST on Online Sales*, OECD Publishing, Paris, https://dx.doi.org/10.1787/e0e2dd2d-en. [1]

OECD (2017), *International VAT/GST Guidelines*, OECD Publishing, Paris, https://dx.doi.org/10.1787/9789264271401-en. [4]

OECD (2017), *Mechanisms for the Effective Collection of VAT/GST*, OECD, Paris, http://www.oecd.org/ctp/consumption/mechanisms-for-the-effective-collection-of-vat-gst.htm. [5]

OECD (2014), *Tax Compliance by Design: Achieving Improved SME Tax Compliance by Adopting a System Perspective*, OECD Publishing, Paris, https://dx.doi.org/10.1787/9789264223219-en. [9]

OECD Forum on Tax Administration (2020), *Code of Conduct: Co-operation between tax administrations and sharing and gig economy platforms*, OECD, Paris, http://www.oecd.org/tax/forum-on-tax-administration/publications-and-products/code-of-conduct-co-operation-between-tax-administrations-and-sharing-and-gig-economy-platforms.pdf (accessed on 25 February 2021). [7]

OECD/Council of Europe (2011), *The Multilateral Convention on Mutual Administrative Assistance in Tax Matters: Amended by the 2010 Protocol*, OECD Publishing, Paris, https://dx.doi.org/10.1787/9789264115606-en. [8]

Notes

[1] See also similar considerations in a working paper by Milanez, A. and B. Bratta (2019) developed under the WP2 auspices on *Taxation and the future of work: How tax systems influence choice of employment form,* (Milanez and Bratta, 2019[10]).

[2] It is recognised that the VAT/GST status of the sharing/gig economy actors is determined in line with the relevant provisions of each national legislation and does not fall within the scope of this work.

[3] For the purposes of this report, a financial intermediary is a third party that processes payments in relation to the supplies by the underlying sharing/gig economy suppliers. These financial intermediaries are distinct from sharing/gig economy platforms that establish contact between the underlying suppliers and users and allows the provision of a sharing/gig economy supply. Collection and reporting roles for these sharing/gig economy platforms are considered under Section 3.3.

[4] See further Forum on Tax Administration's publication on *Tax compliance by design* (2014) that assembles the different elements of technology associated with modern commerce into a system (as

an integral part of the one SMEs use to carry out their daily business) that delivers a seamless and secure flow of accurate tax information and tax payments (OECD, 2014[9]).

5 The OECD Model Rules define a "Seller" as a Platform user that is registered at any moment during the Reportable period with the platform for the purposes of the provision of Relevant Services. In this light, Sellers can include both individuals and Entities. For the purposes of this report the term "Seller" is used interchangeably with the term "Provider" (OECD, 2020[3]).

4 Compliance risk and enforcement measures to support VAT/GST policy and administration responses to the sharing/gig economy

This chapter provides a high-level overview of a number of compliance risk management and enforcement strategies that tax authorities may wish to consider as part of their overall VAT/GST strategy for the sharing/gig economy. It discusses the role of risk-based compliance management and of data collection and exchange; the importance of inter-agency cooperation and of the international cooperation between tax authorities; and the design of a sanctions policy that imposes real consequences of non-compliance for non-compliant actors.

4.1. Introduction

Chapters 2 and 3 of this report present an overall approach for the design of a jurisdiction's VAT/GST strategy for the sharing/gig economy and a range of policy options for tax authorities to consider in implementing such a strategy, taking into account their specific national circumstances and key policy motivations. This chapter complements that analysis with a high-level overview of a number of compliance risk management and enforcement strategies that tax authorities may wish to consider as part of their overall VAT/GST strategy for the sharing/gig economy.

These strategies will need to be embedded in jurisdictions' overall compliance and enforcement strategies, notably to ensure an even VAT/GST playing field between the sharing/gig economy and competing sectors in the traditional and broader platform economy. Such a broad approach to VAT/GST compliance and enforcement will also be necessary to avoid sharing/gig economy providers and other actors adjusting their activities or mode of operation to avoid VAT/GST obligations (i.e. ensure a "no place to hide" approach).

This chapter first discusses the role of risk-based compliance management in VAT/GST strategies for the sharing/gig economy and the critical role of data collection and exchange in this context. It then discusses the importance of inter-agency cooperation and of the international cooperation between tax authorities. It concludes with a brief discussion on the design of a sanctions policy that imposes real consequences of non-compliance for non-compliant actors.

4.1.1. Risk-based compliance management

Management of VAT/GST compliance in the sharing/gig economy will almost inevitably need to rely on a risk-based management approach. The number of actors involved in the sharing/gig economy make a case-by-case handling practically impossible. Such a risk-based approach will need to rely on effective risk profiling of the various sharing/gig economy actors, based on risk indices notably indicating the possible revenue risk involved, the possible impact on the integrity of the tax system and the likelihood of the risk materialising. These risk indicators and the associated risk profiling may need to be adjusted according to the sector of the sharing/gig economy and in light of the jurisdiction's VAT/GST policy strategy. It is reasonable to expect that tax authorities' may wish to focus their efforts first on the sectors/types of supplies of the sharing/gig economy that require the most immediate VAT/GST policy attention given their impact on VAT/GST revenue and/or the impact of an uneven VAT/GST treatment on competitive neutrality.

The implementation of such a risk-based compliance management strategy will need to be based on the efficient collection of data on the relevant sharing/gig economy sector(s) and robust data analytics. In light of the heavy reliance of the sharing/gig economy on technology and on digital data to carry out their commercial activities, the use of technology by tax authorities to collect data from sharing/gig economy actors (including via information sharing roles for digital platforms) is likely to boost their risk-based compliance management capacity. The use of information technology to collect VAT/GST relevant data by tax authorities is notably discussed in section 3.2.5 of this report.

Financial information elements will necessarily play an important role in tax authorities' risk-based VAT/GST compliance strategy for the sharing/gig economy. The financial flows reflect the actual transactions carried out and efficient risk analysis and tax auditing in a highly automated and digitalised industry such as the sharing/gig economy will highly depend on the automated cross-checking of information, including financial flows. It will thus be important for tax administrations to have access to financial information for the efficient management of VAT/GST compliance in the sharing/gig economy. Section 3.2.6 of this report discusses the possible introduction of reporting obligations on financial intermediaries in the sharing/gig economy, which could serve to support tax authorities' risk-based compliance management approaches in addition to facilitating overall compliance and administration.

Information held by tax authorities for other tax purposes than VAT/GST as well by other national agencies (see section 4.1.2 below) could also be of potential use. In particular, the information collected and exchanged under the OECD Model Reporting Rules (discussed under section 3.3.4. of this report) is likely to present considerable opportunities for VAT/GST risk identification and management (OECD, 2020[1]). Targeted audit and monitoring activities, such as mystery shopping by the tax administration on specific platforms, can further enhance the effectiveness of tax authorities VAT/GST compliance strategies.

The OECD's Forum on Tax Administration has produced a series of guidance material and reports[1] for tax authorities to draw on in implementing risk analysis solutions which are based on practical experience in countries.

These approaches may enable national administration to adopt a targeted and proactive rather than a reactive response to compliance risks in combination with an overall strategy that facilitates VAT/GST compliance for legitimate sharing/gig economy operators.

4.1.2. Co-operation and information exchange amongst domestic agencies

To increase the efficiency of their systems in analysing considerable amounts of data from different sources, tax authorities could consider implementing measures to facilitate co-operation and information exchange amongst domestic public agencies. These could notably include social security authorities, property registers, road traffic authorities, financial intelligence units etc. These data can be of considerable use for a tax authority to identify unregistered digital economy business activity. For example, data held by a financial intelligence unit to counter anti-money laundering and counter-terrorism financing has already been useful in certain jurisdictions for the detecting of non-compliance in the sharing/gig economy by allowing the tax administration to trace funds flowing to non-compliant sharing/gig economy actors (e.g. drivers and lessors of properties) from overseas banks to local banks from where they are distributed. In jurisdictions that apply a registration requirement for properties that are offered for vacation rental, these registration data can also be useful for tax authorities.

4.1.3. Imposing real consequences on non-compliant actors

To safeguard the level playing field with compliant operators, tax authorities may wish to complement their VAT/GST compliance strategy with a well-balanced sanctions policy that imposes real consequences of non-compliance for non-compliant actors (residents and non-residents). Such real consequences could involve, depending on the case, the publication of lists of non-compliant actors (a "naming and shaming" approach); deterring interaction by platforms and/or uses with non-compliant actors; imposing proportionate monetary penalties; using payment service providers and other financial intermediaries as a backstop to deal with no compliance, notably by blocking payments on accounts belonging to non-compliant sharing/gig economy actors.

As a last resort, jurisdictions may consider the possibility of implementing stricter sanctions such as blocking access to platforms or applications deployed by non-compliant actors. This may be considered as the ultimate resource of reaction when all other compliance tools have been exhausted. Tax authorities will need to ensure that such an intrusive measure is permissible from a broader legal and regulatory perspective, including in a jurisdiction's trade and broader international context, and consult with Internet service providers on the technical and operation aspects. While experience shows that non-compliant actors may find ways to circumvent such a measure by using alternative internet domains, the public announcement of a sharing/gig economy website blocking by a jurisdiction's authorities may serve as a deterrent for users.

Overall, tax authorities will need to ensure that a sanctions policy for VAT/GST non-compliance in the sharing/gig economy is properly balanced and proportionate, notably by allowing sufficient time for non-compliance to be addressed and by safeguarding the possibility to appeal against a sanction.

The enforcement of sanctions against non-resident actors is likely to require the appropriate international administrative cooperation. This is discussed in the next section below.

4.1.4. Leverage the international administrative cooperation

The importance of the exchange of information and other forms of international administrative co-operation for jurisdictions' VAT/GST compliance strategies targeted at the sharing/gig economy has been highlighted throughout this report. The need for international cooperation between tax authorities can notably be expected as sharing/gig economy platforms may often have no physical presence in the jurisdiction of taxation and this may also be the case for the underlying providers in a number of sectors as this economy continues to evolve (e.g. in cooperative finance). This section outlines a number of possible tools that may serve as a basis for such international administrative cooperation.

The *International VAT/GST Guidelines* present the existing tools available to tax authorities for both multilateral and bilateral co-operation (OECD, 2017[2]). They point to the possibilities for multilateral co-operation through the *Multilateral Convention on Mutual Assistance in Tax Matters*[2] which was developed jointly by the OECD and the Council of Europe in 1988 and amended by Protocol in 2010. This Convention and Protocol are in principle applicable also to VAT/GST and provide for a wide range of forms of administrative co-operation between the parties in the assessment and collection of taxes, in particular with a view to combatting tax evasion and avoidance. This is particularly relevant as notably platforms facilitating sharing/gig economy supplies can increasingly access markets in other jurisdictions without having a physical presence thereat. This can also be relevant for sharing/gig economy providers of services remotely from another jurisdiction.

The *International VAT/GST Guidelines* (OECD, 2017[2]) also highlight the possibilities of bilateral co-operation, in particular through the exchange of information provisions of Article 26 of the *OECD Model Tax Convention* (MTC) (OECD, 2017[3]). This may offer an appropriate basis for the exchange of information between tax authorities both in individual cases and in broader classes of cases in respect of VAT/GST. Bilateral tax treaties may thus provide a possible mechanism for enhanced co-operation and development of solutions to common problems. In this context, the *International VAT/GST Guidelines* also point to the possibilities offered by the OECD *Model Agreement on Exchange of Information.*[3]

The OECD *Model Rules for Reporting by Platform Operators with respect to Sellers in the Sharing and Gig Economy* is the most recent tool that has become available to tax authorities to support the exchange of information specifically targeted at the sharing/gig economy (OECD, 2020[1]). Section 3.2.4 of this report discusses how the information exchanged under this instrument can contribute to jurisdictions VAT/GST compliance strategies in respect of the sharing/gig economy. Tax authorities are strongly encouraged to use these Model Reporting Rules as a basis for their information collection and exchange policies, notably to ensure international consistency and minimize risks of duplication in reporting requirements (OECD, 2020[1]). This will notably be important to facilitate compliance by sharing/gig economy platforms that are likely to face reporting obligations in multiple jurisdictions.

Overall, the exchange of information is likely to be a priority for the international administrative cooperation in respect VAT/GST compliance in the sharing/gig economy, notably to allow the parties involved in sharing/gig economy activity to be identified, to monitor volumes and values of transactions, to assess the VAT/GST liabilities involved and compliance with the obligations to report and remit the proper amounts of VAT/GST on these transactions. Assistance in recovery of taxes may be necessary in certain case as well a proper mechanism to resolve disputes, as appropriate.

References

OECD (2020), *Model Rules for Reporting by Platform Operators with respect to Sellers in the Sharing and Gig Economy*, OECD , Paris, https://www.oecd.org/tax/exchange-of-tax-information/model-rules-for-reporting-by-platform-operators-with-respect-to-sellers-in-the-sharing-and-gig-economy.htm (accessed on 25 February 2021). [1]

OECD (2017), *International VAT/GST Guidelines*, OECD Publishing, Paris, https://dx.doi.org/10.1787/9789264271401-en. [2]

OECD (2017), *Model Tax Convention on Income and on Capital: Condensed Version 2017*, OECD Publishing, Paris, https://dx.doi.org/10.1787/mtc_cond-2017-en. [3]

Notes

[1] Please see more on a series of guidance material and reports by the OECD's Forum on Tax Administration available at http://www.oecd.org/tax/forum-on-tax-administration/publications-and-products/.

[2] Please see further information on the Convention on the dedicated webpage: https://www.oecd.org/tax/exchange-of-tax-information/convention-on-mutual-administrative-assistance-in-tax-matters.

[3] The OECD *Model Agreement on Exchange of Information* is available at http://www.oecd.org/ctp/exchange-of-tax-information/2082215.pdf.

Annex A. Other relevant OECD work on sharing and gig economy

Caveat: please note that this box does not attempt to provide an exhaustive list of all sharing/gig economy related work that have been or are being carried out by different directorates within the OECD, but summarises those that are potentially relevant from both tax and other broader policy perspectives.

Tax administration

- *The Sharing and Gig Economy: Effective Taxation of Platform Sellers* (2019): this report by the OECD Forum on Tax Administration looks at approaches to help ensure the effective taxation of those earning income from the sharing and gig economy with key focus on the direct tax aspects. It considers the different ways/options that tax administrations can best engage with platform sellers, sharing and gig economy platforms, and each other to enable more effective tax compliance. Based on these options, the report further identifies recommendations and areas for future work: joint work between tax administrations and platforms on providing information and support to platform sellers on their tax obligations, which includes further consideration of a possible model Code of Conduct; improving the evidence base to enhance understanding of the tax at risk, which includes consideration of enhanced international cooperation as well as continued exchange of information on successful practices and legislative approaches; and assisting in the possible development of a legislative model for standardised reporting by sharing and gig economy platforms. Particularly, the recommendation on the development of standardised reporting model has resulted in a 2020 report on *Model Rules for Reporting by Platform Operators with respect to Sellers in the Sharing and Gig Economy* (please see Annex C for more details on this report). This report contains the OECD's Model Rules that require digital platforms to collect information on the income realised by those offering accommodation, transport and personal services through platforms and to report the information to tax authorities. Although the focus is on direct taxes, the report recognises the potential relevant use of the information reported for VAT/GST purposes. Full copies of these two reports are available at http://www.oecd.org/ctp/the-sharing-and-gig-economy-effective-taxation-of-platform-sellers-574b61f8-en.htm and https://www.oecd.org/tax/exchange-of-tax-information/model-rules-for-reporting-by-platform-operators-with-respect-to-sellers-in-the-sharing-and-gig-economy.htm, respectively.

Broader policy implications

- *Gig Economy Platforms: Boon or Bane?* (2019): this working paper by the OECD economics department (please note that this is not an official publication but a working paper) analyses the economic and social implications of the emergence of gig economy platforms. For the purposes of the paper, the gig economy platforms are defined as two-sided digital platforms that match workers on one side of the market to customers (final consumers or businesses). Based on this definition, platforms involved in facilitating accommodation services are excluded as they do not intermediate labour. As the paper explores various policy implications, it highlights some challenges associated with labour market policy such as ongoing legal controversies surrounding platform worker classification issues (self-employed contractors or platform employees) and the need for ensuring adequate working conditions (access to basic social protection, including work-related accidents, parental benefits, health and pensions) and incentives for skill upgrading for platform workers. The paper also recognises the need for appropriate tax policy responses in the area and makes a reference to the ongoing WP9 work on the sharing/gig economy for VAT/GST implications. Full copy of the paper is available at https://www.oecd-ilibrary.org/economics/gig-economy-platforms-boon-or-bane_fdb0570b-en

- *OECD Tourism Trends and Policies 2016*: the report by the OECD Centre for Entrepreneurship, SMEs, Regions and Cities (CFE) in partnership with the European Commission is a biennial publication included in the programme of work of the OECD Tourism Committee. The report has a dedicated chapter on policy implications for the tourism sharing economy (transportation, accommodation, travel and dining experiences) in which challenges associated with areas such as consumer protection, taxation and regulation are highlighted with some examples of policy responses from different countries. Specifically, these challenges include competitive imbalances, with prospect of unfair competition for traditional regulated businesses, labour market risks and protection for drivers, hosts and other service providers and taxation of sharing economy activities and impact on tax revenues. The report notes that the initial policy responses vary across different jurisdictions and most of them take 'wait and see' approach. Other government / industry responses include review of existing rules and regulations, introduction of licensing and permit systems, direct engagement and promotion and self-regulation with platforms introducing quality controls, standards and insurance systems, etc. In the area of taxation, the report recognises that the platforms may play a more active role in providing clarity around tax obligations and supporting compliance, or even directly by collecting tax (e.g. accommodation tax) on behalf of hosts. Full copy of the report is available at https://www.oecd-ilibrary.org/industry-and-services/oecd-tourism-trends-and-policies-2016_tour-2016-en
- *OECD Tourism Trends and Policies 2020*: in addition to the 2016 report, the 2020 report undertaken in co-operation with the European Union, highlights sharing economy associated challenges faced by governments, particularly negative impacts of the growth of the sharing accommodation activities in relation to consumer protection and ensuring a level playing field with similar accommodation businesses. The report provides some examples of government responses that include local authorities' introduction of regulations to limit the number of days allowed for short-term rentals, restrictions on second-home rentals and measures involving digital platforms such as information reporting requirements to the tax authorities. Again, the report emphasises the importance of acquiring accurate data on the development of the sharing economy to better understand its impact on the tourism economy. In this context, it notes certain efforts being made, notably through data sharing with platforms. The report also indicates that administrative sources such as accommodation providers' VAT registration details also offer potential in this area. Full copy of the report is available at https://www.oecd.org/cfe/tourism/oecd-tourism-trends-and-policies-20767773.htm

Monitoring and measurement

- *Measuring platform mediated workers* (2019): as part of the OECD Digital Economy Papers series by the OECD Directorate for Science, Technology and Innovation (STI), this paper, recognising challenges in estimating the number of platform workers, reviews different attempts made by private agencies and official statistical agencies to measure platform workers and offers recommendations on how to improve the measurement in the future (i.e. how to use different forms of surveys / how to formulate the survey questions to obtain desired outcomes). Full copy of the paper is available at https://www.oecd-ilibrary.org/science-and-technology/measuring-platform-mediated-workers_170a14d9-en

Source: OECD

Annex B. Potential COVID-19 impact on the sharing and gig economy sectors

At the moment of the finalisation of this report, restrictions to contain and mitigate the spread and infection rate of the Covid-19 virus were still in place in countries around the world. While it is clear that the pandemic and the necessary containment and mitigation measures taken by governments worldwide have triggered a deep global economic recession, which has undoubtedly also affected the sharing/gig economy activity, it is unclear at the time of completion of this report what the actual impact of the pandemic will be on the sharing/gig economy. This annex outlines a number of emerging observations based on anecdotal evidence from publicly available sources (cited below) and consultation with sharing/gig economy representatives at the time of the finalisation of the report.

- Overall, jurisdictions will need to continue monitoring the economic impact of the pandemic, including the impact on the sharing/gig economy, and adjust their policy responses accordingly as appropriate.
- It remains difficult to anticipate and estimate the medium- and longer-term impact of the COVID-19 crisis on economic growth and activity, let alone on the sharing/gig economy specifically. It is clear, however, that the outbreak of the pandemic and the lockdown and social distancing measures introduced in countries worldwide to stop the virus from spreading have notably caused significant disruptions to the economic sectors that involve physical contact and movement of people in the public space. This has inevitably impacted activity in what are currently the largest sectors of the sharing/gig economy, i.e. the sectors of transportation ("ride-sourcing") and of short-term accommodation (real-estate rental).
- On the other hand, new habits have developed in response to the COVID-19 outbreak that are likely to have a positive impact on certain types of sharing/gig activity, such as online teaching; delivery of food and other items sold online; provision of non-traditional types of short-term accommodation as people are not comfortable staying in traditional hotels or resorts; short-term rental of online working space…. Growth in sharing/gig economy activity that responds to behavioural changes from the COVID-19 outbreak may (have) offset some of the loss of activity in other sharing/gig economy sectors.
- To some extent, the platforms that generate and facilitate sharing/gig economy activity may be in a better position to weather the COVID-19 crisis than their competitors in the traditional industries, as they may have more flexibility in managing their costs and risks. This may apply in particular to the larger sharing/gig economy platforms operators, which continue to have access to finance. The situation may be more challenging for smaller and/or start-up platforms. Sharing/gig economy platform operators may however also attract additional attention from investors that may wish to tap into the capacity of this economy to respond to new consumer needs and changes in people's behaviour during and after the crisis. Some sharing/gig economy platforms, including smaller ones, became a lifeline for traditional businesses in certain sectors (e.g. restaurants) adapting to new ways of continuing to serve their customers. It is unlikely that these businesses will stop using these new, technology-based distribution

channels after the crisis. This could also provide opportunities for small(er) sharing/gig economy platforms to survive and grow.

- Similarly, it could be expected that (even) more people may look to supplement their income after the crisis including by monetising their skills and assets via sharing/gig economy activities.
- Overall, it can be expected that a number of (new) habits developed during the pandemic will continue after the pandemic. For example, a share of the population may continue embracing the "live-and-work-anywhere" mind-set that has grown during the pandemic and this may lead to an increase demand in rental of short-term accommodation as people that have the flexibility to work from anywhere may want to do so from many different locations.
- Even as the coronavirus changes people's lifestyles, early studies among consumers appear to be optimistic about the future of the sharing/gig economy in the long run. Research in the United States has for instance suggested that only about 25% of users might stop using sharing/gig economy services post- COVID-19 in the absence of a vaccine (which has meanwhile become available).

Sources:

https://www.statista.com/statistics/1110632/sharing-economy-services-united-states-covid19/

https://medium.com/swlh/coronavirus-the-end-of-the-sharing-economy-or-a-new-beginning-a142acbb7130

https://economictimes.indiatimes.com/small-biz/startups/features/the-sharing-economy-faces-the-abyss-in-a-pandemic/articleshow/74857984.cms?from=mdr

https://www.verisk.com/insurance/covid-19/iso-insights/sharing-economy-reacts-to-covid-19-outbreak/

https://thebluecircle.co/2020/05/08/impact-on-shared-economy-in-the-covid-19-era/

https://www.nytimes.com/2020/05/07/technology/the-results-are-in-for-the-sharing-economy-they-are-ugly.html

https://www.japantimes.co.jp/news/2020/05/28/business/coronavirus-sharing-economy/#.XvDhQqYUnmQ

https://telecoms.com/504717/can-the-sharing-economy-survive-covid-19/

https://calibreresearch.com/report/global-sharing-economy-market-9436

http://www.china.org.cn/business/2020-03/07/content_75784902

https://3wnews.org/tag/gig-economy-and-sharing-economy-market-impact-of-covid-19/

Annex C. Model rules for reporting by platform operators with respect to sellers in the sharing/gig economy – Key features

The OECD has developed the Model Rules for Reporting by Platform Operators with respect to Sellers in the Sharing and Gig Economy (hereafter the Model Rules) which were approved by the OECD/G20 Framework on BEPS on 29 June 2020. To allow the swift and coherent implementation of the Model Rules, the OECD worked (is working) on the international legal and technical framework to facilitate the automatic exchange of the information collected under the Model Rules between tax administrations, (which is expected to be completed in the second half of 2020). The full text of the rules is available at *www.oecd.org/tax/exchange-of-tax-information/model-rules-for-reporting-by-platform-operators-with-respect-tosellers-in-the-sharing-and-gig-economy.htm*

This Annex provides an overview of the key features and architecture of the Model Rules.

- **The Model Rules foresee a targeted scope of transactions to be reported so as to enhance adequacy and efficiency. They enable targeted reporting in respect of (both entity and individual) Sellers from the rental of immovable property and provision of transportation, delivery and other personal services (other than those provided by a seller pursuant to an employment relationship with the Platform Operator).** By ensuring that the Model Rules capture only certain types of services and that the information is made available to the jurisdiction(s) in which there is likely to be a tax impact, the rules seek to address as a matter of priority the (direct) tax compliance risks posed by such activities in light of their scale, the income they generate and the profile of the Sellers involved. The Model Rules recognise however that as digital markets are rapidly evolving and other types of transactions may become relevant, the scope of the Model Rules may need to be expanded as appropriate. It is irrespective of whether such services are provided directly by third party sellers or users or whether the platform first purchases such services and then offers these services in its own name to users. These services are collectively referred to as Relevant Services for the purposes of the Model Rules. The Model Rules feature exclusions for services performed by governmental entities, large hotel operators and providers of scheduled publicly-accessible transportation (such as railroads and bus services).
- **Entities that contract with Sellers to make available the Platform are in principle subject to the Model Rules when they are resident, incorporated or managed in the jurisdiction adopting the Model Rules**. **The term Platform** does not include software exclusively allowing the processing of payments, listing or advertising or redirecting or transferring of users to a Platform with respect to the Relevant Services. There are optional exclusions (i.e. at jurisdictions' discretion) for small-scale platforms operators (with aggregate consideration at the level of the Platform over the previous year less than EUR 1 million) and platforms that do not allow the Sellers to derive a profit from the consideration received or that do not have Reportable Sellers.

- **A two-step information flow is foreseen: the information is first reported to the tax administration of the jurisdiction of residence of the Reporting Platform Operator, which then exchanges the information with the Reportable Jurisdiction in which the Seller is resident or where the immovable property is located.** The rules require annual reporting to tax authorities of the jurisdiction of residence by 31 January of the year following the Reportable Period. They also require that the platform operators provide their sellers with an information statement of the amount of the consideration they have earned through the platform as well as any fees, commissions and taxes paid or withheld.
- **To enable effective taxpayer matching, the Model Rules foresee the reporting of a Seller's name, primary address, Tax Identification Number (including a VAT/GST Registration Number issued by the jurisdiction of the Primary Address of the Seller) and date of birth**. The Model Rules also foresee the possibility to confirm the identity and tax residence of a Seller through a so-called government verification service. In the context of rental of immovable property services the Model Rules require that the address of the property as well as wherever available the land registration number and type of each property listing (e.g. hotel, apartment, parking space) as well as the number of days each property listing was rented are reported.
- To support tax compliance activities and, where possible, prefilling of tax returns**, jurisdictions will also receive information on the types of services provided and the income earned by the Seller during each quarter of the reportable period and the number of such Relevant Service in which this consideration was paid or credited.** Consideration is the amount net of any fees, commissions or taxes withheld or charged by the Reporting Platform Operator. The information with respect to the consideration and other amounts must be reported in respect of the quarter in which those amounts have been paid or credited. Where the consideration is refunded after the reporting deadline, for instance in case of cancellations of transactions the Reporting Platform Operator is expected to submit a corrected report reflecting any relevant changes. Moreover procedures are foreseen to avoid duplicate reporting in cases involving multiple Platform Operators in respect of a single Platform.
- **The Model Rules provide due diligence and reporting rules that ensure that accurate information gets reported without imposing overly burdensome procedures on Platform Operators**. Generally the verification of the information collected and reported needs to be done by the Platform Operator by using all records available to it including information already collected for AML/KYC purposes, as part of its on-boarding or re-documentation procedures, for payment purposes or other commercial or regulatory ends.
- **The Model Rules work on the basis that the jurisdiction implementing the Model Rules will be, in principle, interested in receiving information in respect of Sellers resident in their jurisdiction.**
- **With respect to cases where the Platform Operator is resident in a jurisdiction that has not implemented the Model Rules or is not an exchange partner of the jurisdiction implementing the Model Rules and therefore the information cannot be obtained from a Partner Jurisdiction**, the Model Rules recognise the possibility that a jurisdiction may want to impose local reporting on platforms in the jurisdiction in which Sellers are resident or where immovable property being rented is located.
- **The Model Rules provide a reporting regime that can also be used for other tax-related purposes such as indirect taxes, local taxes and social security contributions,** provided this is permitted under the relevant international exchange agreement.

Annex D. Overview of business models of the accommodation and transportation sectors

This Annex provides a description of the main business models of the (currently) two largest sectors of the sharing/gig economy: accommodation and transportation sectors. These two sectors serve as pilot cases for the relevant analysis in this report. This approach resonates with the assumption that these two sectors are likely to create the most urgent pressure on VAT/GST policy in jurisdictions worldwide and are thus likely to be the first to require policy and/or administrative action from a VAT/GST perspective.

In this context, this Annex presents an overview of the key features of the main business models operated in these two sectors that are likely to be relevant from a VAT/GST perspective. This includes a general description of each sector, main business models including payment modalities, platform governance and trust mechanisms, economic importance of each sector and available information elements.

These descriptions are based on the features of the major platforms that currently account for the majority of market share in these sectors. These are inevitably snapshots of the current state of play that is likely to change rapidly as the sharing/gig economy continues to evolve.

Accommodation sector

General description

In general, the accommodation sector can be broadly divided into different sub-sectors based on the accommodation types such as hotels & motels, serviced apartments and short-term (vacation) rentals, etc. In the sharing/gig economy context, it is often understood to mainly refer to short-term (vacation) rentals while the scope is expanding to comprise other accommodation types as well. For the purposes of the analysis in the report, the focus is on short-term rentals sector, which comprises a majority of the accommodation related sharing/gig economy activities.

In fact, the concept of short-term rental has been around for a long time similar to the hotel industry. However, this particular sector has seen major changes in the past decade with the advent of digital platforms – experienced approximately 167% market size growth from 2010 to 2018 (Skift research, 2019[1]). Typically, the platform connects potential guests with professional or non-professional hosts offering accommodation services. Furthermore, the platform may provide other services either on their own name or on behalf of other platforms and/or third parties (see below *Business Models* for more details).

The short-term rental sector ecosystem

While the underlying accommodation types may vary, the short-term rental is the prevalent type of the accommodation related sharing/gig economy activities. Notably, the digital platforms play a key role in this space and much of the focus has been on them as they have largely contributed to the rapid growth of the sector. However, it is also important to understand that there is an entire ecosystem of different players as shown in Figure A D.1. below. As technology has become more affordable and accessible, many different stakeholders are increasingly benefitting from the growth of the short-term rental sector.

For illustration purposes, Box A D.1. below briefly describes some of the main players in this ecosystem (see also Figure A D.1. for a graphic illustration of interactions of these actors).

Box A D.1. Description of the main players in the short-term rental sector ecosystem

- **The platforms and metasearch engines**: although the market is predominantly driven by the major platforms that generally operate across multiple jurisdictions, there is a growing interest from metasearch engines to enter the market, adding short-term rental search functionality in partnership with some of the platforms or independent property managers. They act as an intermediary and redirect customers to the partnering booking sites, channel managers, etc.
- **Independent hosts**: evidence suggests that approximately more than half of all short-term rental properties are those from individual hosts or small-time property managers with less than ten properties. Most of them operate through the platforms, benefitting from easy access to a wider group of potential customers, secure payment facilities and other support services offered by the platforms. Some of them also purchase services from B2B vendors such as key drop-off services and home cleaning. Additionally, there are individuals who turn to professional property managers to take care of the rentals on behalf of them (see below *Professional Agents* under *Business Models*).
- **Host service providers**: host service providers refer to those providing management services such as listing, cleaning and pricing. They often operate 'behind-the-scenes' without guests knowing that the property is managed by a company rather than a homeowner itself. However, to strengthen and protect their brand identity, some of them recently choose to show that they are managing the properties on platforms by stating in the property description or showing their logo next to the property listing. They let the property owners pick and choose the services they want to outsource and charge commissions.

- **Traditional holiday home managers**: holiday home managers who have appeared as owners of second homes in holiday destinations often live far away to manage the property themselves. In recent years, the technological developments have allowed these holiday home managers to move into the online space and expand their business. Today, some of them even manage hundreds and thousands of properties through their own branded platforms. Similar to the platforms, they operate both the commission-based model and subscription model while the latter is more popular.
- **Branded home managers**: they provide an end-to-end service for both property owners and guests. As the brand is important, they only work with homes that meet their standards and they are likely to work with hotel companies as well as major platforms. Recently, investment has gone into the master-lease companies that focus on purpose-built or converted multi-unit buildings partially or wholly leased for short-term rental purposes. However, this development is currently more prevalent in the U.S.
- **B2B vendors**: with the advancement of technology, the opportunities for the B2B vendors are fast growing in the short-term rental space. They provide different types of services such as property management software, marketing solutions, website/app building, revenue management, etc.

Figure A D.1. The short-term rental sector ecosystem

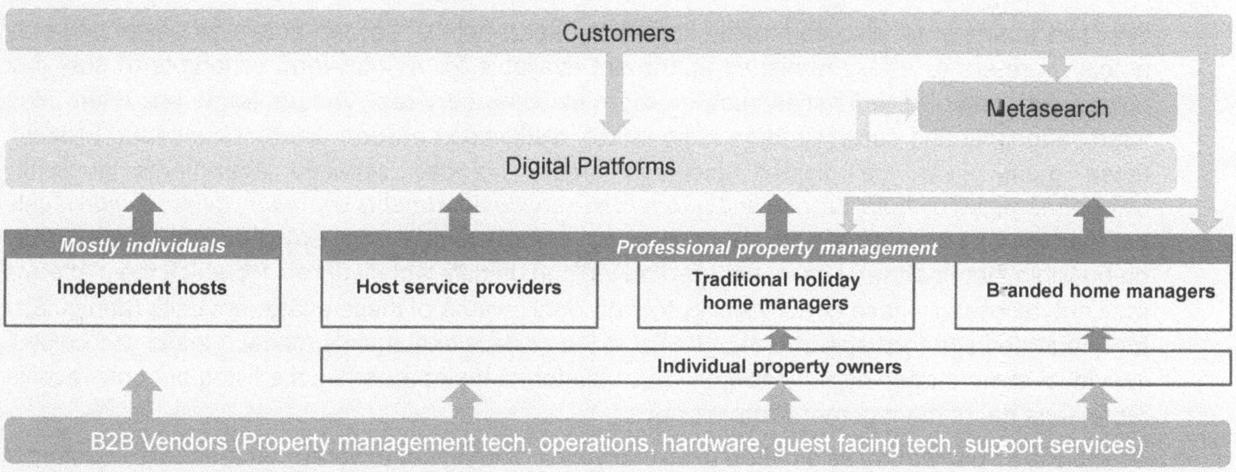

Source: Skift research (2019), *The Short-Term Rental Ecosystem and Vendor Deep Dive* (Skift research, 2019[1])

Business models

In understanding different business models operating in the sector, it is important to highlight the essential role of digital platforms in bringing together different players in the ecosystem. Whether it is short-term rentals or other types of accommodation (e.g. serviced apartments), the platforms are at the centre of the scene in the sharing/gig economy space. Broadly, main business models involving these platforms can be categorised into four types depending on the nature of the underlying supply and the type of consideration involved (e.g. monetary or in-kind). Please note that the distinction between "pure" accommodation and 'accommodation combined with other services' may not be always clear-cut and the latter model is increasingly employed by large platforms in the sector.

- **"Pure" accommodation**: the platform facilitates renting out whole or part of an individual's primary or secondary residence to other individuals. However, the platform increasingly offers other types of accommodation such as serviced apartments.

- **Accommodation combined with other services**: in addition to "pure" accommodation services (as described above), the platform may also provide other services such as vacation experiences (e.g. food tours, concerts), restaurant reservation services, car-hires, air travels, etc.
- **Exchange of houses**: the platform brings together individuals (platform users) who agree to exchange houses (i.e. to travel and stay in each other's primary or secondary residence). Usually, the users pay membership fees to subscribe to the platform and transact with each other.
- **Couchsurfing**: the platform provides a place where individuals come together and agree to stay in each other's house in return for non-monetary consideration (e.g. cook dinner as a token of gratitude).

Emerging trends in business models

The major trends in the development of business models in the accommodation sector include an expanding scope of the accommodation types used for short (and/or long) term rentals such as serviced apartments. Another important development relates to the involvement of different actors (e.g. other platforms and/or third parties) in the supply chain that would allow the platforms to further expand their service offerings including non-sharing/gig economy supplies such as air travels, car rentals, and insurance services.

- Serviced apartments: also commonly known as "apart-hotels", "condo hotels" or "extended-stay hotels", it refers to a fully furnished apartment available for a short-term or long-term stay that comes with hotel-like amenities such as room cleaning services. Various terms are often used interchangeably and currently there is no official distinction between different concepts. Broadly, these models can be divided into two types: branded serviced apartments generally owned/managed by hotel brands and unbranded service apartments owned by different individuals but managed by an intermediary agent or property management company. For both cases, it may be possible that apartment units are listed/advertised on different platforms for which the platforms may not necessarily have direct visibility to individual owners of these apartment units (particularly for unbranded serviced apartments). Similar to the professional agents model (please see below), individual owners often do not know on which platforms their properties are listed but only receive rental fees net of management commissions.
- "Platforms on platforms": as an effort to diversify their offerings and thereby increase their customer base, (traditional) digital platforms such as online travel agency companies list properties originally offered by other platforms on their platforms. Once the customer identifies a property they would like to book, they are redirected to the original platform's website to conclude the transaction. Similarly, the platforms may allow other platforms to make their (different) service offerings accessible on their platforms (e.g. car reservation website accessible through accommodation platforms). The hosting platform may receive commissions from other platforms based on the number of referrals made or do it for free as part of their marketing strategy. Where these multiple platforms are involved in the supply chain, the hosting platform may not always have direct visibility as to who the underlying supplier (i.e. property owner) is similar to the professional agents model described below. In addition, the platforms increasingly expand their services to include those of third party companies such as car rentals, air travel and insurance services, some of which may not necessarily fall within the scope of sharing/gig economy activities.
- Professional agents: individuals may contract with professional property management agents/companies to list and/or advertise their properties on different accommodation platforms. These individuals often do not know on which platforms their properties are listed but only receive rental fees net of management commissions from the agents/companies.

Payment models

Payment facilities is an important feature of the platform services in the sharing/gig economy context, and the platforms may choose to operate different payment models for various economic, social and commercial reasons. Generally, the accommodation provider (i.e. hosts) charges a rental fee and the guest pays it either directly to the provider or through the platform. Additionally, the platform collects commission from either the provider, the guest or both. Variations of these payment models may include (see further below *Graphic illustration of basic operation of these models*):

- *Model 1*: A platform may collect x% commission from providers and y% service fee from users. The user pays the entire amount (e.g. rental fee and service fee) up front to the platform; the platform then pays the provider net of commission and service fee.
- *Model 2*: A platform may charge x% transaction fee (commission) to the providers only; the users pay no fee. The user pays to the provider the amount agreed who subsequently remits the x% fee to the platform.
- *Model 3*: A platform may charge x% transaction fee (commission) to the providers only; the users pay no fee. The user pays to the platform the amount agreed who subsequently pays the provider net of the x% fee.
- *Model 4*: A platform does not charge any fees to the provider and the user. The platform provides a place where the provider and the user can contact each other, but the underlying transaction is carried out only between the provider and the user without involvement of the platform. The platform's revenue comes from advertisements displayed on the platform.
- *Cash transactions*: it is rare in the accommodation sector but possible in *Model 2* where the user may pay cash directly to the provider. The platform would subsequently receive its commission from the provider either by adding it to the provider's periodic subscription fees to the platform or by asking the provider to remit it to the platform periodically.
- *New payment modalities*: mobile payment solutions such as mobile wallets are increasingly used in developing economies where a large portion of the population have limited access to formal financial services. Other technology-enabled payment solutions are emerging as well, including the use of digital assets (e.g. some platforms in the accommodation sector are considering accepting a specific type of digital asset (bitcoin) in certain regions of the world) that may become more popular in the coming years.

Graphic illustration of basic operation of the models

Figure A D.2. Model 1 - the platform collects service fee from guests (users) and commission from hosts (providers)

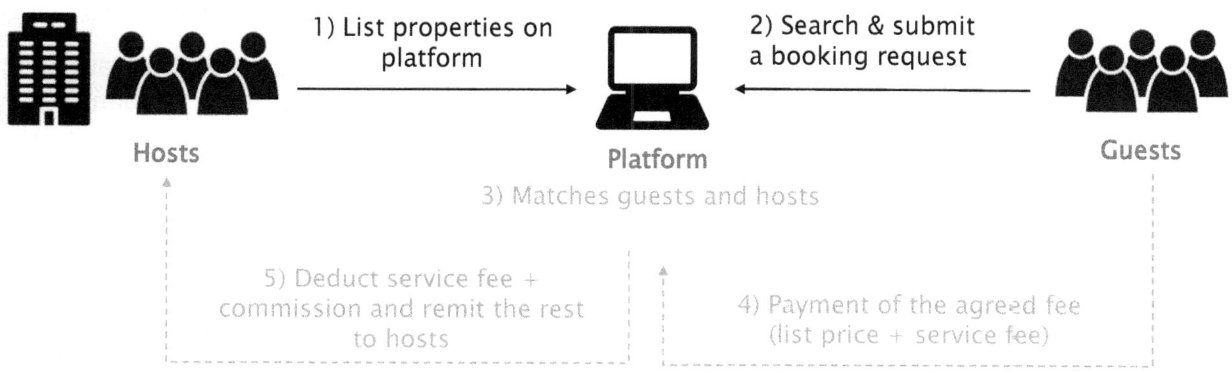

Source: OECD analysis

Figure A D.3. Model 2&3 - the platform collects commission only from hosts (providers)

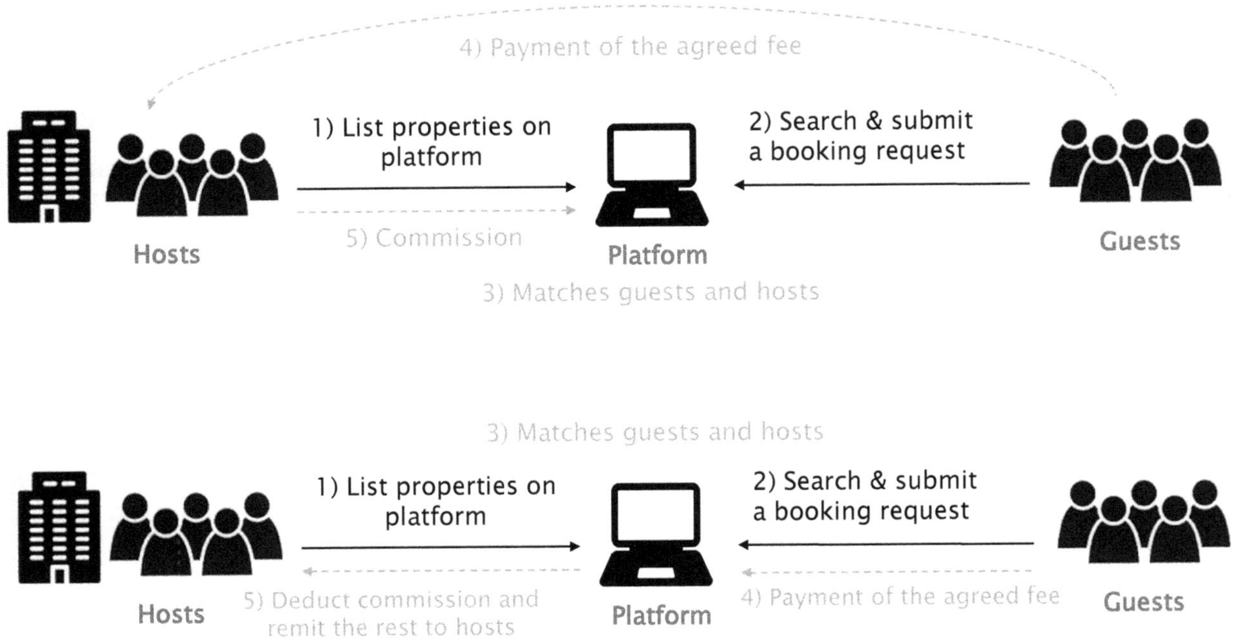

Source: OECD analysis

Figure A D.4. Model 4 - the platform generates revenue from advertisements

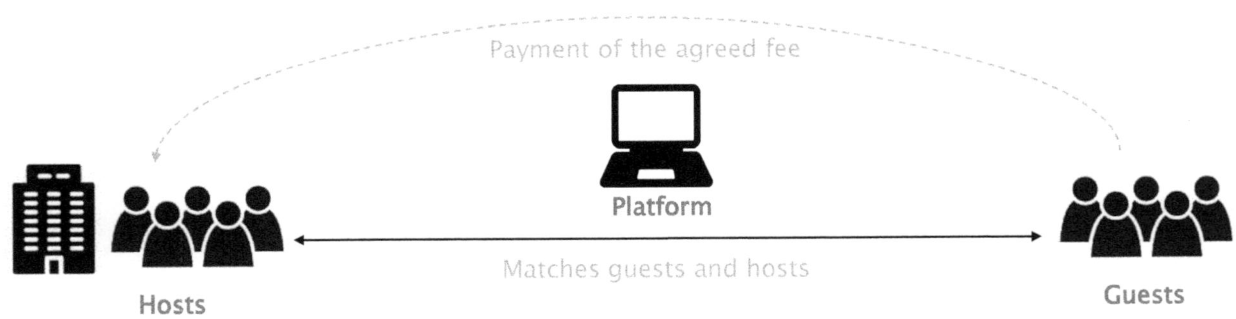

Source: OECD analysis

Platform governance and trust

Effective platform governance that enables safe exchanges between strangers and thereby cultivates trust is critical for a platform's success (Hagiu and Rothman, 2016[2]). In order to foster trust, a platform usually operates various institutional and legal governance mechanisms that may include: pre-screening procedure (including some physical in-site visits to the buildings), cross-review system, secure payment processing services, formulation of rules and standards regarding service levels and provision of civil liability insurance and guarantees to protect assets and users (Akbar and Tracogna, 2018[3]). Furthermore, the platform may offer other ancillary services such as photography services and a template to help hosts to post their offers in an effort to further streamline the service offering and improve user experience.

- **Pre-screening procedure**: the platform may limit access to the platform to only specific assets and resources that meet predefined quality standards (Wirtz et al., 2019[4]). The platform may also perform some in-site visits to the property to verify that the property exists and meets necessary security standards. Similarly, the platform may require users to go through identification verification process (e.g. matching of a photo in a government issued ID with another photo of an individual) to be able to access the platform service.

- **Reviews/ratings**: hosts and guests can evaluate each other. In certain cases, the platform may cancel a reservation or suspend the listing of a particular host where the host's performance rating shows a trend of unusually low scores and negative comments. In extreme cases where a bad review is the result of serious safety related issues (e.g. crimes), the platform may automatically remove or deactivate the user's account.
- **Pricing**: the platform may provide recommended prices (i.e. price range) for hosts calculated by internal pricing algorithm based on multiple factors such as demand, season and local events.
- **Payment processing services**: the platform operates a system where the payment made by a guest is released after the guest checks in to ensure that the property exists.
- **Customer support**: In addition to an online help centre that allows hosts and guests to get answers about frequently asked questions in an automated way, the platform may provide further assistance in resolving disputes between a host and a guest.
- **Insurance/guarantees**: the platform offers a guarantee to the hosts for the damages incurred in their property while providing accommodation services. If a guest insists that the damage was already there before the guest used the property, the platform may decide to compensate the host for the damage.
- **Other services**: the platform may provide tutorial materials (e.g. online guidelines) or links to the relevant government agency's website to educate their users to comply with regulatory obligations (e.g. tax). In addition, the platform may voluntarily provide a periodic summary of the transactions to the providers in an effort to help them comply with their tax obligations, if any.

Size and growth of the sector

Evidence suggests that the accommodation sector is one of the two largest sectors in terms of value of transaction. In Europe, the sector comprises approximately 50% of the total market value[1] and is projected to more than double its size by 2025 in Southeast Asia[2] (European Commission and PwC UK, 2016[5]) (Google, Temasek and Bain & Company, 2019[6]). When it comes to the short-term rental market size, estimates provide that the global consumer market for short-term rentals has reached USD 107 billion in 2018 (see Figure A D.2 below for the global accommodation market composition – although overlaps between different accommodation types exist in the short-term rental sector, it shows that a majority of the market value comes from the sharing/gig economy related short-term rentals) (Skift research, 2019[1]). Moreover, as the market is further dominated by major players, top five players are estimated to account for approximately 73% of all gross bookings in the sector in 2019 compared to only 4% in 2010 (Skift research, 2019[1]).[3]

Figure A D.5. Global accommodation market (in Billions USD)

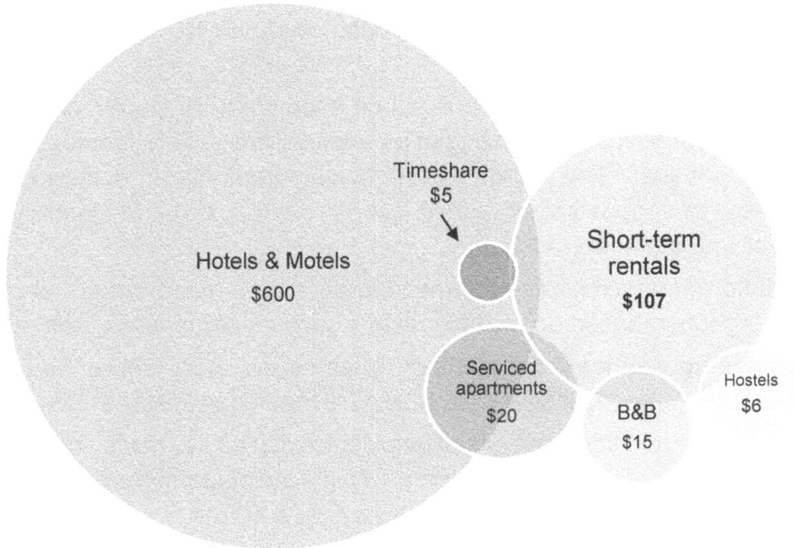

Source: Skift research (2019), *The Short-Term Rental Ecosystem and Vendor Deep Dive* (Skift research, 2019[1])

Convergence of business models

As the sector evolves, different segments are increasingly converging with one another and the line is blurring between different accommodation types and providers. In order to remain competitive, traditional accommodation providers such as hotels are entering the short-term rental market, and online travel agents have also started to expand their offerings to include apartment rentals and homestays. Respondents from incumbent players vary: adopting features of platforms by launching a booking app, launching competing platforms, and acquiring the platforms. Similarly, the platforms are expanding their services and becoming resembling their traditional counterparts establishing stronger brand identity (e.g. the platform moving towards owning and controlling its own room inventory). Furthermore, as the platform's services expand, customer demand is pushing them towards hotels, with greater standardisation and more whole-unit rentals (as opposed to a room in one's home). These trends lead to vertical market integration, diminishing the difference between the sharing/gig economy platforms and "traditional" economic operators.

Information elements

Through various governance and trust ensuring mechanisms as described above, the sharing/gig economy platforms operating in the accommodation sector typically collect the following information (please note that the below is not an exhaustive list. It is also acknowledged that, depending on a business model of the platform, a particular platform may not collect all of the information listed below):

- User account details (name, email address, phone number)
- Identification information (including tax ID number)
- Transaction value
- Residency address of hosts
- Property address
- Payment information (bank account details)

The platforms generally have mechanisms in place to verify the accuracy of the information collected, which could include using technology-based solutions (e.g. artificial intelligence) to verify property listings.

Transportation Sector

General description

In the sharing/gig economy context, the transportation sector generally refers to a segment in which the platform connects drivers, which may include non-professionals in the sense that these drivers do not possess professional permits (e.g. taxi medallion) other than a legitimate driver's license, with passengers, often private individuals, for either a short or long distance trip.

Business models

Main business models that currently operate in the sector may include:

- **Ride-sourcing**: this generally refers to app-based ride-sourcing services (often short distance). The service focuses on providing taxi/car-like services but the platforms may provide different types of transportation means such as motorcycles, bikes, electronic scooters, boats and ferries. Cross-border trips are very rare, notably due to logistical and regulatory complications (e.g. high-risk liability insurance related coverage issues, time consuming/costly border procedures, etc.).
    - "Platforms on platforms": instead of purchasing/maintaining their own inventories, the ride-sourcing platform may offer other transportation means (e.g. e-scooters or bikes) owned by other platforms on their platform.
- **Ride-sharing/car-pooling**: the platform matches drivers who have spare capacity in their cars and plan to drive particular (long distance) routes with passengers who want to travel on the same or similar routes including cross-border trips.
- **Driveway/parking sharing**: the platform connects drivers with (more often) individuals who own unused parking spaces for a fee.
- **On-demand delivery**: particularly in light of COVID-19 impact, as the demand for home delivery of essentials, goods and food is increasing, the platforms are further expanding their food (meal) delivery business model into the delivery of grocery and other products, either through acquisition of existing players in the market or through partnership (contractual arrangement) with these players. In these cases, the platform either utilise its existing network of drivers to facilitate the delivery services or provides customers access to the services offered by others while not being directly involved in the delivery. For example, in the food (meal) delivery context, the platform connects drivers, restaurant owners and customers for the delivery of a meal. The platform may either connect restaurants with drivers or connect customers with restaurants that have their own couriers through contractual arrangements. Similarly, in the grocery delivery case, the platform connects drivers, grocery stores (platforms) and customers either by connecting grocery stores with its drivers or by connecting customers with grocery stores that employ their own shoppers to prepare the order and fulfil the delivery service as well.

Payment models

Payment facilities is an important feature of the platform services in the sharing/gig economy context, and the platforms may choose to operate different payment models for various economic, social and commercial reasons. Generally, the provider (i.e. drivers) charges a fee and the user (i.e. passengers) pays it either directly to the provider or through the platform. Additionally, the platform collects commission from either the provider, the user or both. Typically, the major platforms in the transportation sector charge commission only to the providers. Variations of these payment models may include (see further below *Graphic illustration of basic operation of the models*):

- *Model 1*: A platform may collect x% commission from providers and y% service fee from users. The user pays the entire amount (e.g. driving fee and service fee) to the platform; the platform then pays the provider net of commission and service fee.
- *Model 2*: A platform may charge x% transaction fee to the providers only; the users pay no fee. The user pays to the provider the amount agreed who subsequently remits the x% fee to the platform.
- *Model 3*: A platform may charge x% transaction fee to the providers only; the users pay no fee. The user pays to the platform the amount agreed who subsequently pays the provider net of the x% fee.
- *Cash transactions*: cash is the preferred means of payment in certain countries, notably developing countries where people have limited access to the formal financial services. In *Model 2*, if the user pays cash directly to the provider, either the provider could later deposit x% fees to the platform's account or the platform could take x% fees from the provider's credit card portion of the transactions.
- *New payment modalities*: mobile payment solutions such as mobile wallets become increasingly popular and may replace cash transactions in developing countries. Other technology-enabled payment solutions are emerging as well, including the use of digital assets that may become popular in the coming years.

Graphic illustration of basic operation of the models

Figure A D.6. Ride-sourcing model

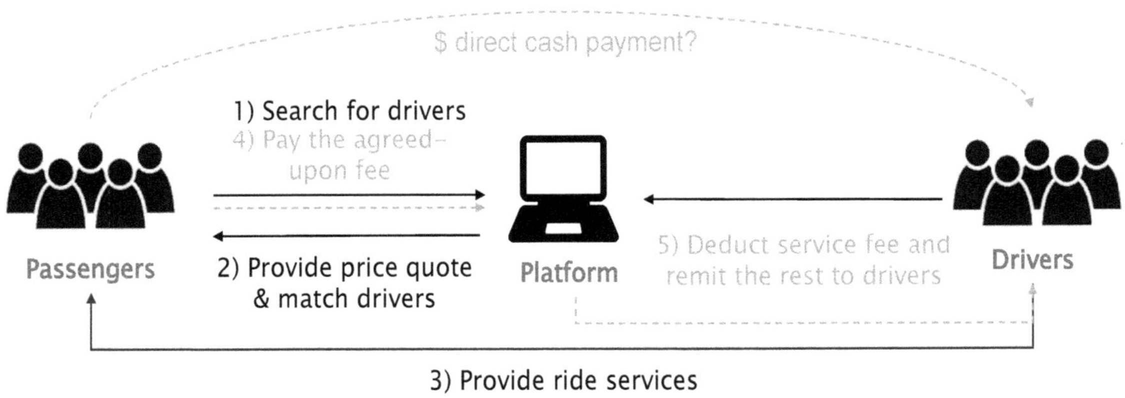

Source: OECD analysis

Figure A D.7. Ride-sourcing model variation 1

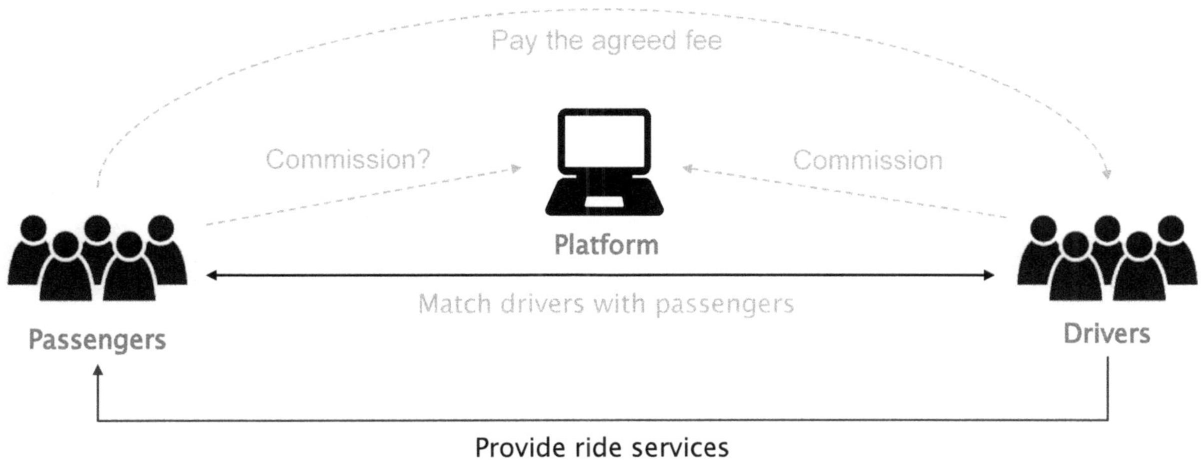

Note: it is clarified that this variation describes the case in which the platform may receive commission from passengers as well. Typically, the platform charges commission only to its drivers but it may be possible that it charges commission to both drivers and passengers.
Source: OECD analysis

Figure A D.8. Ride-sharing/car-pooling model

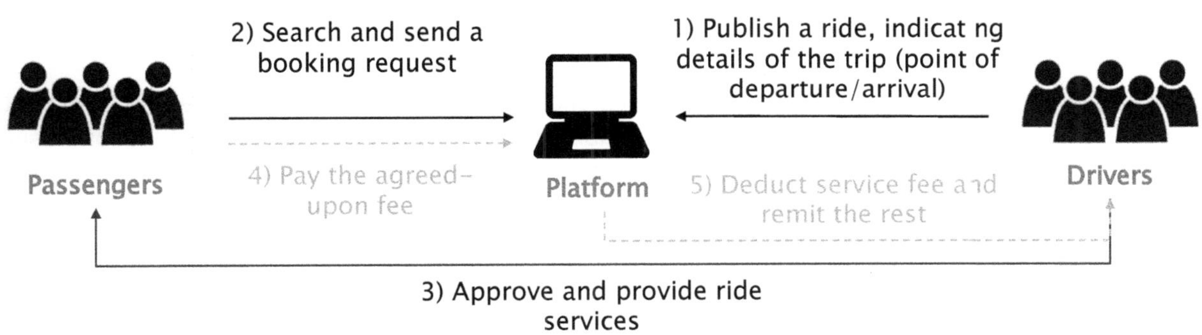

Source: OECD analysis

Figure A D.9. Food (meal) delivery model

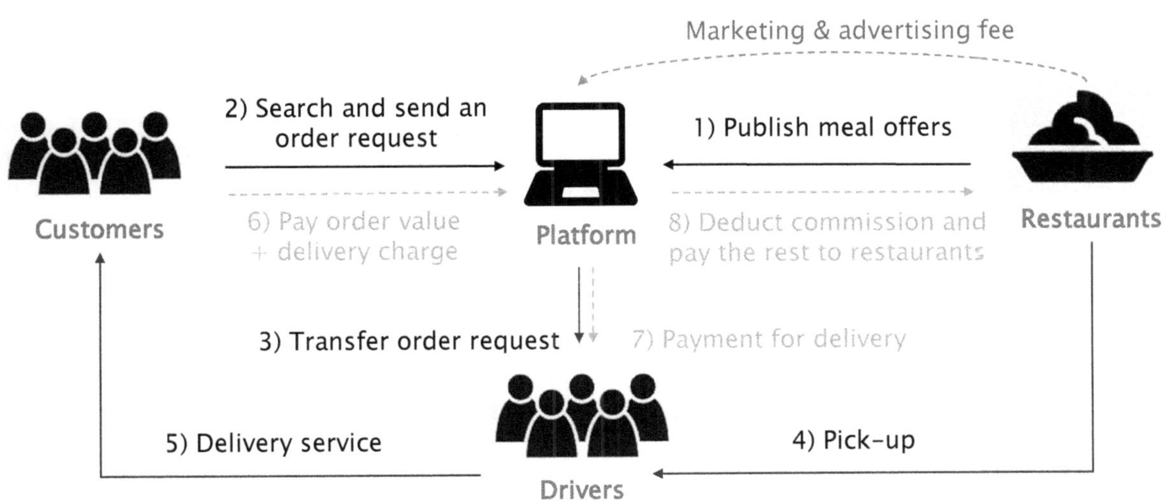

Source: OECD analysis

Figure A D.10. Food (meal) delivery model variation 1 - Restaurant's own couriers

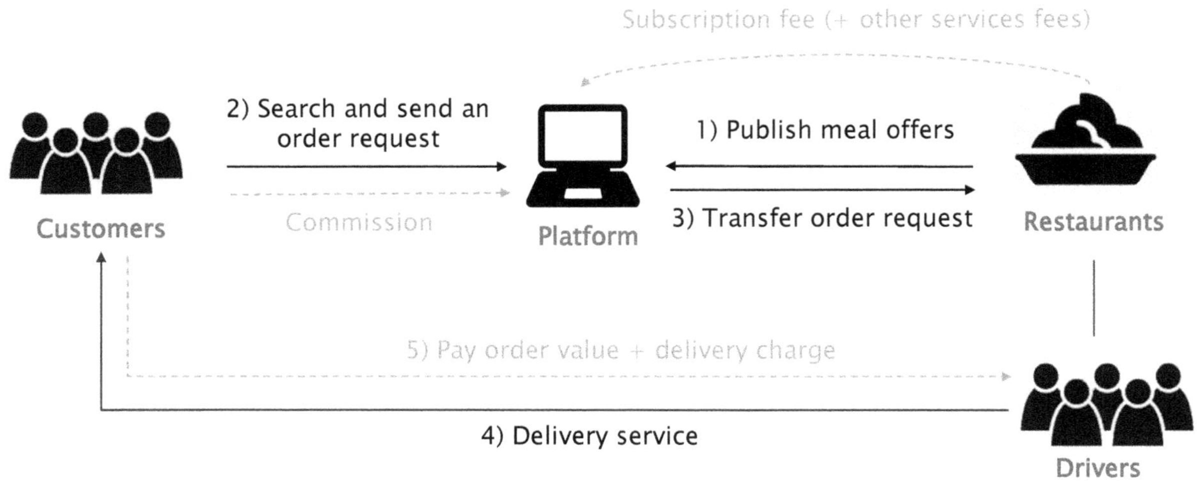

Source: OECD analysis

Platform governance and trust

Effective platform governance that enables safe exchanges between strangers and thereby cultivates trust is critical for a platform's success (Hagiu and Rothman, 2016[2]). In order to foster trust, a platform usually operates various institutional and legal governance mechanisms that may include: pre-screening procedure (including driver's license verification), cross-review system, secure payment processing services, formulation of rules and standards regarding service levels and enhanced safety features (Akbar and Tracogna, 2018[3]).

- **Pre-screening procedure**: the platform may limit access to the platform to only specific assets and resources that meet predefined quality standards (e.g. vehicle requirements). Similarly, the platform usually asks the drivers to provide their driver's license or other equivalent certificate/license (certain jurisdictions may require professional license in order for an individual to engage in passenger transport services for profit) during the subscription process.
- **Reviews/ratings**: drivers and passengers can evaluate each other. In extreme cases where a bad review is the result of serious safety related issues (e.g. crimes), the platform may automatically remove or deactivate the user's account.
- **Pricing**: the platform may provide a price quote calculated by its internal pricing algorithm based on changes in supply and demand, and the drivers may be asked to respect it. Depending on the business model, drivers may be allowed to set their own prices based on recommendation by the platform or the prices may be set on predefined categories rather than on dynamic adjustments. In the case of the ride-sharing/car-pooling business model, the platform may provide recommended prices based on fixed amount per distance. Drivers are free to choose their own but there is usually a price-cap rule to prevent drivers from making profits.
- **Payment processing services**: the platform usually provides secure online payment processing services collecting driving fees from passengers and periodically remitting the fees minus commission to the drivers.

- **Safety features**: in response to recent passenger safety related issues, the platform is moving towards enhancing safety features on the platform such as launching of a "panic button" which both passengers and drivers may press when they feel they are in danger and an alert would be sent to the platform and the police. The platform may also perform more thorough examination of drivers' track records.
- **Other services**: the platform may provide tutorial materials (e.g. online guidelines) or links to the relevant government agency's website to educate their drivers to comply with regulatory obligations (e.g. tax). In addition, the platform may voluntarily provide a periodic summary of the transactions to the drivers in an effort to help them comply with their tax obligations. The platform may also provide invoicing services on behalf of their drivers.

Size and growth of the sector

Evidence suggests that the transport sector is one of the two largest sectors in terms of value of transaction and platform revenue. In Europe, the sector generates approximately 47% of the platforms revenue[4] and is expected to reach USD 40 billion of market value by 2025 in Southeast Asia[5] (European Commission and PwC UK, 2016[5]) (Google, Temasek and Bain & Company, 2019[6]).

Figure A D.11. Gross market volume by sector (in Billions USD, 2018)

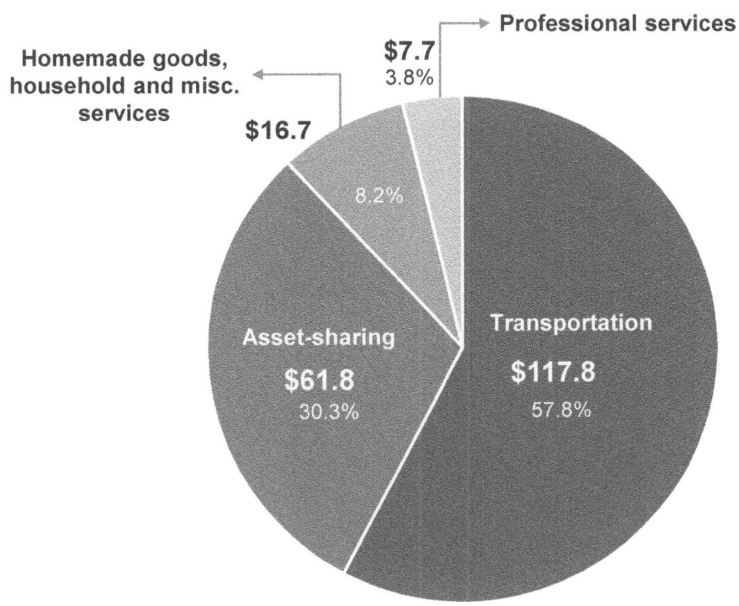

Source: Mastercard & Kaiser Associates (2019), *The Global Gig Economy: Capitalising on a ~$500B Opportunity* (Mastercard and Kaiser Associates, 2019[7])

Information elements

Through various governance and trust ensuring mechanisms as described above, the sharing/gig economy platforms operating in the transport sector typically collect the following information (please note that the below is not an exhaustive list. It is also acknowledged that, depending on a business model of the platform, a particular platform may not collect all of the information listed below):

- User account details (name, phone number)
- Identification information of drivers, including driver's license, tax ID numbers

- Transaction value
- Vehicle information
- Payment information (bank account details)
- Information on trips made (starting and ending points)

The platforms generally have mechanisms in place to verify the accuracy of the information collected. For example, platforms may ask the service providers to pre-fill an information form as part of the on-boarding process and compare it with the information contained in other documentation (e.g. match tax ID provided with the one shown in other certificates).

Annex E. A list of functions considered relevant for the application of the full VAT/GST liability regime (2019 Report on the Role of Digital Platforms in the collection of VAT/GST on Online Sales)

A non-exhaustive list of functions considered relevant for enlisting digital platforms under the full VAT/GST liability regime

This table provides a non-exhaustive list of examples of functions that have been considered relevant by existing regimes for the eligibility of digital platforms for the full VAT/GST liability regime.

Examples of functions that may trigger the eligibility of digital platform for the full VAT/GST liability regime	Examples of functions that may exclude digital platform from eligibility for the full VAT/GST liability regime
• Controlling and/or setting the terms and conditions of the underlying transactions (e.g. price; payment terms; delivery conditions, etc.) and imposing these on participants (buyers, sellers, transporters…);	• Only carries content (e.g. makes only the Internet network available for carrying content via Wi-Fi, cable, satellite, etc.); or
• Direct or indirect involvement in the payment processing (either directly or indirectly through arrangements with third parties, collect payments from customers and transmit these payments to sellers less commissions; obtain pre-authorisations or submit payment instructions or information to the platform's own or to a third-party payment platform or to a platform stipulated in the terms and conditions set by platforms);	• Only processes payments; or
• Direct or indirect involvement in the delivery process and/or in the fulfilment of the supply (incl. influencing/controlling the conditions of delivery; sending approval to suppliers and or instructing a third party to commence the delivery; providing order fulfilment services with or without warehousing services);	• Only advertises offers; or
• Providing customer support services (returns and/or refunds/assistance with dispute resolution).	• Only operates as a click-through/shopping referral platform. Such a platform only transfers via software, an Internet link or otherwise a potential customer to the website of a seller, thus enabling the discovery, promotion or listing of goods for sale by a seller. Customer and seller complete the transaction without any direct or indirect involvement of the digital platform in the setting of the terms of the underlying supply or in the payment or delivery process. Where such a platform's fee is, however, calculated on the basis of the final consideration agreed between the customer and the underlying supplier, this may be an indication of an involvement in the underlying transaction that could bring the digital platform within the scope of the regime.

Source: OECD research

References

Akbar, Y. and A. Tracogna (2018), "The sharing economy and the future of the hotel industry: Transaction cost theory and platform economics", *International Journal of Hospitality Management*, Vol. 71, http://dx.doi.org/10.1016/j.ijhm.2017.12.004. [3]

European Commission and PwC UK (2016), *Assessing the size and presence of the collaborative economy in Europe*, https://op.europa.eu/en/publication-detail/-/publication/2acb7619-b544-11e7-837e-01aa75ed71a1 (accessed on 25 February 2021). [5]

Google, Temasek and Bain & Company (2019), *e-Conomy SEA*, https://www.blog.google/documents/47/SEA_Internet_Economy_Report_2019.pdf (accessed on 25 February 2021). [6]

Hagiu, A. and S. Rothman (2016), "Network effects aren't enough", *Harvard Business Review*, Vol. 94/4, pp. 64-71. [2]

Mastercard and Kaiser Associates (2019), *The Global Gig Economy: Capitalizing on a ~$500B Opportunity*, Mastercard and Kaiser Associates, https://newsroom.mastercard.com/wp-content/uploads/2019/05/Gig-Economy-White-Paper-May-2019.pdf (accessed on 25 February 2021). [7]

Skift research (2019), *The Short-Term Rental Ecosystem and Vendor Deep Dive*, Skift research, https://research.skift.com/report/the-short-term-rental-ecosystem-and-vendor-deep-dive-2019/ (accessed on 25 February 2021). [1]

Wirtz, J. et al. (2019), "Platforms in the peer-to-peer sharing economy", *Journal of Service Management*, Vol. 30/4, http://dx.doi.org/10.1108/JOSM-11-2018-0369. [4]

Notes

[1] For the purposes of the study, the accommodation sector refers to 'households sharing access to unused space in their home or renting out a holiday home to travellers'.

[2] The reference in the report is on online vacation rentals.

[3] The report's estimate includes short-term rentals not only through the digital platforms but also via offline bookings, travel agents, and local connections.

[4] For the purposes of the study, transportation sector refers to 'individuals sharing a ride, car or parking space with others'.

[5] The report includes ride-hailing and food delivery in measuring the market value.

www.ingramcontent.com/pod-product-compliance
Ingram Content Group UK Ltd.
Pitfield, Milton Keynes, MK11 3LW, UK
UKHW051241300926
15471UKWH00015B/1466

9 789264 798168